Practical Guide to
SAP® OpenUI5

Prem Manghnani, Seshu Reddy
& Sheshank Vyas

Thank you for purchasing this book from Espresso Tutorials!

Like a cup of espresso coffee, Espresso Tutorials SAP books are concise and effective. We know that your time is valuable and we deliver information in a succinct and straightforward manner. It only takes our readers a short amount of time to consume SAP concepts. Our books are well recognized in the industry for leveraging tutorial-style instruction and videos to show you step by step how to successfully work with SAP.

Check out our YouTube channel to watch our videos at
https://www.youtube.com/user/EspressoTutorials.

If you are interested in SAP Finance and Controlling, join us at
http://www.fico-forum.com/forum2/
to get your SAP questions answered and contribute to discussions.

Related titles from Espresso Tutorials:

► Michal Krawczyk: SAP® SOA Integration – Enterprise Service Monitoring
  http://5077.espresso-tutorials.com

► Kathi Kones: SAP® List Viewer (ALV) – A Practical Guide for ABAP Developers
  http://5112.espresso-tutorials.com

► Anurag Barua: First Steps in SAP® Fiori
  http://5126.espresso-tutorials.com

► Jelena Perfiljeva: What on Earth is an SAP® IDoc?
  http://5130.espresso-tutorials.com

► Paul Bakker & Rick Bakker: How to Pass the SAP® ABAP Certification Exam
  http://5136.espresso-tutorials.com

► Raquel Seville: SAP® OpenUI5 for Mobile BI and Analytics
  http://5173.espresso-tutorials.com

► Robert Burdwell: First Steps for Building SAP®UI5 Mobile Apps
  http://5176.espresso-tutorials.com

Prem Manghnani, Seshu Reddy & Sheshank Vyas
Practical Guide to SAP® OpenUI5

ISBN:	978-1-984023-22-3
Editor:	Karen Schoch
Cover Design:	Philip Esch, Martin Munzel
Cover Photo:	© istockphoto.com # 545664160 Nikada
Interior Book Design:	Johann-Christian Hanke

All rights reserved.

1st Edition 2018, Gleichen

© 2018 by Espresso Tutorials GmbH

URL: *www.espresso-tutorials.com*

Feedback
We greatly appreciate any kind of feedback you have concerning this book. Please mail us at *info@espresso-tutorials.com*.

Table of Contents

Preface

This book progresses step by step, starting with the introduction and basics of ERP and SAP through to a complete overview of UI5. Each chapter contains detailed information on the relevant topics.

The main purpose of publishing this book about Open UI5 is to succinctly transfer knowledge about UI5 technology. SAP UI5 is a client UI technology which utilizes JavaScript, HMTL5 and CSS. UI5 can run in browsers and will be the future technology for many applications.

UI5 technology will help the transition from traditional systems to handheld and mobile devices.

We have added a few icons to highlight important information. These include:

Tips		
	Tips highlight information that provides more details about the subject being described and/or additional background information.	

Videos		
	Go to the homepage of Espresso Tutorials to watch a video.	

Finally, a note concerning the copyright: all screenshots printed in this book are the copyright of SAP SE. All rights are reserved by SAP SE. Copyright pertains to all SAP images in this publication. For the sake of simplicity, we do not mention this specifically underneath every screen-shot.

1 Introduction to OpenUI5

In a study by Stern (2013)[1], it was found that customers use mobile phones more than PCs because they prefer using mobile applications to websites. Moreover, people check their mobile phones over 150 times a day; i.e. once every 6 minutes. With the current rapid advancement in technology and demanding growth of mobile application development, it is highly advisable for companies and organizations to move into mobility. Since most companies have their own websites, most of them have opted for mobile applications as well. This allows them to produce faster IT solutions by having access to data anywhere, anytime. Mobility has improved workflow for businesses; faster processes, closer customer relations and quicker decisions. Recently, SAP also gained a foothold on mobility.

A user interface (UI) is a channel which enables interaction with an application. A channel could be any device such as Windows, phones, tablets, iPads and iPhones. SAP has developed multiple solutions for web application development and one of these is SAPUI5. SAPUI5/OpenUI5 is simple, easy to use and compatible with multiple devices.

In simple terms, the architecture includes a front end, a back end and an intermediate system. The back end is an SAP system which can be CRM, SRM, ECC or HANA, where the data is stored in ABAP objects. As an interface between the front end and back end we have a gateway server called NetWeaver (NW), provided by SAP, where the back-end logic and database queries are written. This gateway converts the data in the application layer into OData with an HTTP call. OData stands for

---

[1] STERN, J. (2013, May 29). *Cellphone Users Check Phones 150x/Day and Other Internet Fun Facts*. Retrieved from http://abcnews.go.com: *http://abcnews.go.com/blogs/technology/2013/05/cellphone-users-check-phones-150xday-and-other-internet-fun-facts/*

Open Data Protocol. It is a widely-used application that not only helps to fetch the data but allows operations to be performed on it.

A developers' job here is to fetch the data and feed it to the gateway. The NetWeaver Gateway generates OData services in the form of XML/JSON view. To access OData, SAP has built-in functions. The developer must create a model and, based on that model, the written script helps to pull the data from SAP OData. With a single HTTP request, you can get both data and Metadata. Here the model is nothing but raw data. In the view, this raw data is displayed on the screen or desktop using SAPUI5/OpenUI5 controls and their methods.

SAPUI5, a JavaScript UI library, is the latest development in SAP which uses markup/scripting languages such as HTML, JavaScript, JQuery and CSS. These languages are more flexible and are supported on both web-browsers and mobile applications thus providing efficient performance and easy accessibility. In addition, Web Dynpro is an SAP UI framework which is used for building web-based applications either using Java or ABAP. However, it lacks functionality for providing support on mobile devices; it doesn't allow client-side validations and it increases the load on application servers, resulting in low performance and limited UI features with no flexibility. A Web Dynpro Application cannot work on both desktops and mobiles. For mobile devices, a new application needs to be developed. For this reason, SAP developed SAPUI5.

To build any web application, libraries are vital. SAP has provided us with their own customized libraries. A library is nothing but a set of controls which can be used to develop a web application. SAP has provided a set of standard libraries such as sap.m, sap.ui.commons, sap.ui.table and many more. Some libraries provide controls that work best on desktops only and others provide controls that work on both desktops and mobile devices. Every control in a library has certain properties, events, aggregations, associations and methods which vary from control to control.

Aggregation allows you to bind the data to the child control to display the data. It represents a parent-child relationship. The control basically acts as a data container. Association enables you to bind data to the control and is independent of the parent-child relationship.

To create applications for desktops or mobile devices, the user needs to be aware of all the controls available in the library and recognize which control is appropriate for the given requirement or scenario; some controls work best on mobile devices as well as desktops, and some might not work at all.

There are several controls in the library which can be used as the root node of a structure and some that cannot. Similarly, there are several controls that can hold the data and some that cannot. Every control can be made as user-friendly as possible using their events and methods. Therefore, the application completely depends on the developers' creativity and knowledge of the controls.

As mentioned above, every control has a set of properties with respective data types out of which some will be defaulted and can be changed depending on the scenario. It is always recommended to read the documentation before using any control in order to understand how it can be used to develop a responsive web application.

The same control can be found in more than one library but the properties might not be the same. Additionally, the development is done using the MVC (Model-View-Controller) design pattern. All the applications are cross-browser compatible.

SAP Fiori is a web application, or collection of multiple web applications, that works efficiently on all platforms and devices. It was introduced in 2013 at the SAP TechEd conference and provides role-based, responsive, coherent and simple applications. Additionally, SAP also provides a productive mobile application development platform known as SMP (SAP Mobile Platform). SMP can be cloud-based and speeds up the delivery and development of business-to-customer and business-to-enterprise mobile applications on any device.

By the end of 2013, SAPUI5 turned itself into an open source development toolkit and became OpenUI5. Since it's an open source, we can find code available at GitHub and perform changes, bug fixes, etc.—all free of charge.

OpenUI5 is similar to SAPUI5, but SAPUI5 is a version that can be only used by SAP customers who have a license. Overall, UI5 consists of rich features and flexible libraries. These features give developers control to build interactive apps, and to sort and filter data. They also provide a huge variety of approximately 200 controls and give access to JSON or XML data from the server side—UI5 is therefore a very valuable tool!

2 OpenUI5—Getting started

The purpose of this chapter is to show OpenUI5 and the installation of the UI development toolkit library, along with the setup of the development environment. The UI toolkit holds a variety of rich user interfaces and elements for modern web-based applications

OpenUI5 uses a 3-digit version identifier (e.g. 1.12.3). The first digit "1" is the major version number. The second digit "12" is the minor version number and the third digit "3" is the patch version number. The latest release is 1.32.11 and provides new functionality for the debugger: UI5 Inspector (covered in later chapters), improved controls and better functionality.

2.1 Libraries in OpenUI5

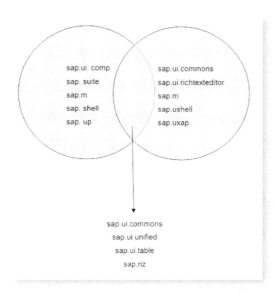

SAPUI5 provides a set of JavaScript and CSS libraries which can be combined and used in an application to increase the functionality. The library combinations have certain guidelines and can be seen in the below figure.

Refer to Figure 2.1 to see the possible correct combinations.

Figure 2.1: UI5 libraries

Libraries listed in the middle area can be combined with libraries listed on the left (e.g. sap.m + sap.ui.table) or with libraries on the right side (e.g. sap.ui.commons + sap.ushell). However, libraries listed on the left side cannot be combined with libraries listed on the right side.

SAPUI5 consists of the latest JS (JavaScript) application programming interfaces (APIs) and can only run on browsers supporting HTML5. Libraries such as sap.ui.core, sap.ui.layout and sap.ui.unified are basic libraries that support all platforms. Commonly used libraries are sap.m for mobile devices and sap.commons for web applications.

Figure 2.2 and Figure 2.3 show the differences when using different libraries.

Figure 2.2 : UI5 sample using sap.m library

Figure 2.3: UI5 sample using sap.commons library

2.2   OpenUI5 development environment

OpenUI5 is a client-side UI technology that runs on a browser using JavaScript, HTML and CSS. Server-side, on the other hand, is responsible for deploying applications, holding UI5 libraries and connecting with databases. *SAP NetWeaver Application Server,* for example, holds UI libraries and makes the libraries available for the client side when receiving a request.

Application development using OpenUI5 is initiated by setting up a development environment in the front-end PC and a UI5 library installed in the backend. Depending on your requirements, you can implement any one of the following:

▶   SAP Web IDE is a well-formulated environment used mainly for developing complex applications. It provides support and functionality on Fiori and mobile hybrid applications, and has a wide range of plugins and templates.

▶ Eclipse tools enable you to develop simple applications. Eclipse IDE provides setup wizards and plugins for support, which make navigation and implementation of code faster.

▶ The SAP HANA Studio Developer Edition is available if you are looking to develop for SAP HANA.

▶ OpenUI5 runtime kit can be installed via *http://openui5.org/ download.html#stableRelease*. Unzip the contents and deploy it on a server such as an Apache HTTPD server (www.apache.org) or refer to the online version of OpenUI5 by typing *https://sapui5. hana.ondemand.com/resources/sap-ui-core.js* in the header section of the main HTML file.

Content delivery network (CDN)

 If you wish to load resources externally, use a content delivery network (CDN). CDN is defined as a system of distributed networks maintained at multiple data centers. Its primary purpose is to provide content to users depending on their geographic location.

2.3 Eclipse installation

An easier way of developing UI5 is by using Eclipse IDE (*http://www. eclipse.org/downloads/*) in addition to the SAP development toolkit (*https://tools.hana.ondemand.com/*) and Apache Server. Before Installing Eclipse, we need to install the latest Java JDK version. Eclipse Luna and Kepler are the versions currently supported for SAP tools, with Luna being the well-revised version.

For Eclipse installation, follow the steps below:

▶ Download Eclipse IDE for java developers—Luna version. Extract all the files from the zip folder and run the eclipse.exe file. A window pops up, asking you to provide your workspace folder path. Workspace is where all your programs, servers and metadata are stored.

▶ After Eclipse, we need to install the SAPUI5 toolkit. On the Eclipse main window (menu bar) click on HELP followed by INSTALL NEW SOFTWARE, as can be seen in Figure 2.4. This opens a pop-up window where you create a repository for storing SAPUI5 toolkit contents and provide appropriate Name and Location (provide URL *https://tools.hana.ondemand.com/luna/* in the location field).

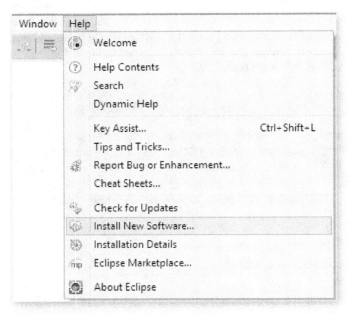

Figure 2.4: Install new software

▶ A list of items appears that are available under that URL. To develop SAPUI5 applications we only require ABAP Development Tools and the UI5 development toolkit for HTML5. If you wish to use UI5 with HANA, you can select SAP HANA tools and the HANA cloud platform. Click on Next and accept the terms. This initiates installation—ignore all the warnings you get.

▶ Figure 2.5 shows how available software can be selected.

Available Software

Check the items that you wish to install.

Work with: SAP Tools - https://tools.hana.ondemand.com/luna/

type filter text

Name	Version
☑ 000 ABAP Development Tools for SAP NetWeaver	
☐ 000 Modeling Tools for SAP BW powered by SAP HANA	
☐ 000 SAP HANA Cloud Integration Tools	
☐ 000 SAP HANA Cloud Platform Tools	
☐ 000 SAP HANA Tools	
☐ 000 SAP Identity Management Tools	
☐ 000 SAP Mobile Platform Tools	
☑ 000 UI Development Toolkit for HTML5	

Select All   Deselect All   7 items selected

Figure 2.5: Select available software

▶ Now we will use the Eclipse wizard to create the application. On the Eclipse main window (menu bar) select FILE • NEW • OTHER. Scroll down and look for SAPUI5 APPLICATION DEVELOPMENT; underneath that, select **Application Project** and click on NEXT (See Figure 2.6). Provide any Project Name and select a Library you would like to use (it is recommended to start your program name with a Z if you wish to upload in the ABAP server). If you prefer to have a view, check CREATE AN INITIAL VIEW.

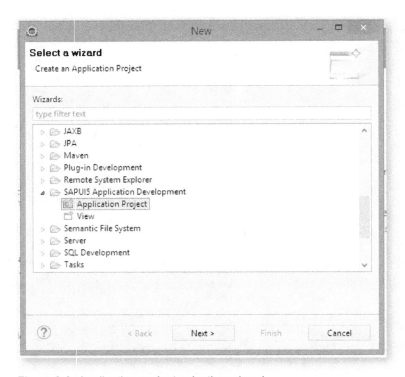

Figure 2.6: Application project selection wizard

▶ As seen in Figure 2.7, you need to provide a name for your view and the type of development paradigm. Then, select JAVASCRIPT and click on FINISH.

▶ You will be presented with all your resources and contents which include view.js, controller.js and html files. Under these files, we have to write code to build the application.

▶ In later chapters, we will learn more about views, controllers and models, and their respective types. The example above is created using a view based on the *MVC (Model-View-Controller)* concept. We can also create an application without a view, but it is not recommended because it makes code management difficult and messy.

Figure 2.7: Create a new view—application project

▶ A server is required to deploy or run your application. There are various options for this such as the *SAP NetWeaver Application Server* (if you have access to SAP), which is recommended. In addition, local servers such as Apache can be used. For this example, let's use a local server on Eclipse.

▶ See Figure 2.8 for the working syntax of Eclipse.

Figure 2.8: Working syntax of Eclipse

► It is very easy to configure a server on Eclipse. In the menu bar click on Windows • Show View • Servers. In the bottom window click on the No servers are available link. A window pops up which consists of a list of servers. Next, select Apache and then select the Tomcat v7.0 server and click on Next. Provide the directory path and click on Download and Install. This creates a new folder under the Project Explorer tab, named Servers.

"Could not load Tomcat…" error solution

If you encounter the error "Could not load the Tomcat…", close Eclipse. Copy all the files from Tomcat/conf folder and paste them in the Workspace/Servers/Tomcat v7.0 Server at localhost-config. Start Eclipse. On the left side, under Project Explorer, right-click on the Server folder and select Refresh.

▶ With this, we have completed our installation. Now it's time to run the application. Under Project Explorer, right-click on PROGRAM NAME and select RUN AS • RUN ON SERVER. (OR) Click on the Run icon (⊙ ▾) shown on the menu bar. Finally select RUN ON SERVER.

▶ Figure 2.9 shows the output in Eclipse.

Figure 2.9 : Eclipse working output

2.4   Chrome development tools

In this section, we will see the debugging of OpenUI5 on a Chrome browser. In addition, we will learn about UI5 Inspector which was released in OpenUI5 version 1.32.

To access the debugger, a basic understanding of development tools in the Chrome browser is required. Figure 2.10 shows how the Chrome development tool looks.

To open debugger, press [F12] or [Ctrl] + [⇧] + [i] on the Chrome browser—this opens a new panel or window in the browser. In the panel, we can see multiple options in the toolbar of the console. The following are the basic functionalities for each option in the toolbar:

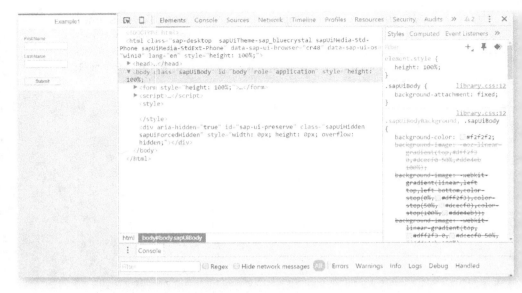

Figure 2.10: Chrome development tool layout

▶ **Elements**—Under this section we find HTML scripts and CSS styles. The main purpose of this is to identify any attribute id's for a particular HTML element and any styles associated to it. Under this panel, we can change element properties, styles and metrics for temporary/testing purposes. The page is arranged in a structured hierarchical manner using DOM interface; clicking on any element displays all the styles, properties and event listeners related to it, on the right side of the panel.

▶ **Console**—This displays all the warnings and errors pointed out in our program. Additionally, we can write JavaScript statements in our live application to apply any change to its workings and behavior.

▶ **Sources**—This shows all the resources our application is requesting and loads them from the server. This section is the one which we use the most after Console. In our case, no matter which code is used, this section displays what we have written in our IDE. This panel is used mostly for the purpose of debugging, using breakpoints on event listeners and analyzing the call stack.

► **Network**—This panel gives a list of all the resources loaded into our application. Named resources, along with detailed descriptions about each resource such as size, type, time to load, etc., are displayed. We can also configure network speeds and types by selecting the appropriate options from the drop-down field at the header level of the panel (default is no throttling).

► **Timeline**—This panel gives an in-depth timing analysis of each operation carried out by an application. From the analysis, it becomes easier to manipulate and sort out elements which take more time, in order to improve performance. Recording options under this panel is one of the most important features.

► **Profiles**—This is also a tool which helps to optimize and improve your code. Here you have ability to maintain separate profiles on execution times and memory usage, for each operation. We have three profile options under this panel: CPU profiler shows execution times for JavaScript functions, Heap profiler shows memory distribution of JS objects and DOM nodes, CSS selector profiler gives aggregated times spent matching selectors to elements in DOM tree.

► **Resources**—This panel allows you to monitor application data stored in AppCache, local storage, cookies or any other predefined database.

► **Audits**—This provides suggestions and optimization steps to improve application performance and decrease loading times. Audits are categorized into Network utilization and web page performance.

2.4.1   UI inspector

As we know, with the availability of sample applications and API references, development has been made simpler by using UI5 Inspector. UI5 inspector is a recent addition to the Chrome development tools; it is free to install and is open source.

To inspect any UI control simply right click on the relevant control and select INSPECT UI5 CONTROL. It highlights the code for that control inside the panel. See Figure 2.11 for steps on inspecting UI elements.

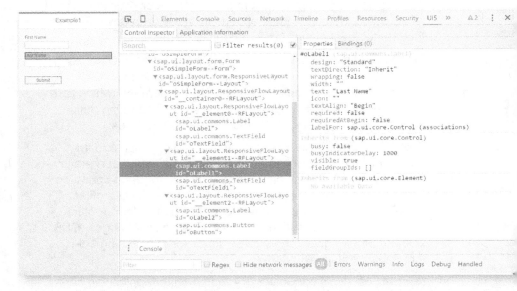

Figure 2.11 : Inspect UI elements

On the right side, you can see a PROPERTIES tab which displays all the properties associated with that control. You can change the properties any time and the UI is updated on-the-spot. The BINDINGS tab shows a description of the model and provides details about bindings, if there are any.

3 OpenUI5 Concepts

OpenUI5 concepts are the main components which help in understanding the structure of OpenUI5.

MVC is a software architectural pattern for implementing UIs. It consists of three units: the model, the view and the controller.

"M" stands for "model", also known as "publisher", and is responsible for managing and providing application data linked to the database level. It accepts requests from the view and responds back to the controller.

"V" stands for "view", or the presentation layer, and is for displaying data to the user. Data is displayed based on the controller's decision, or vice versa; i.e. view receives a user's actions and forwards it to the controller.

"C" stands for "controller" and it takes the user input and performs data model operations, modifications and updates. A controller can hold more than one view.

The reason these units are separated is to implement software code extensibility and reusability, and to distinctly represent data from user interactions. Many developers prefer to use MVC while dealing with user interfaces (UIs).

When MVC is used in web development, *view* acts as a graphical element, *controller* consists of all JavaScript/jQuery coding to process user actions and *model* provides the data required on a controller's request. The architecture of MVC can be seen in Figure 3.1.

Multiple fragments of views can be associated with a single controller. Using different user interface elements or replacing them with another set of interfaces on the same business logic are examples of what can be done. This is what differentiates MVC from other GUI architectures.

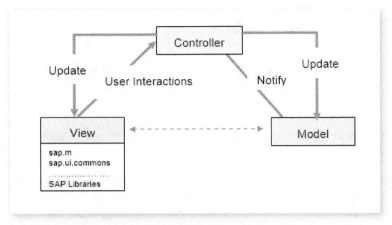

Figure 3.1: MVC architecture

3.1 Bootstrapping

In computer science, a *Bootstrap* is defined as a first piece of code that a program runs on start and is responsible for loading the rest of the components. The process of loading and initializing OpenUI5 in our HTML page is called "bootstrapping". Code is written between the <script> tags—where we specify resources, themes and libraries.

```
1   <!DOCTYPE HTML>
2   <html>
3       <head>
4           <meta http-equiv="X-UA-Compatible" content="IE=edge">
5           <meta http-equiv='Content-Type' content='text/html;charset=UTF-8'/>
6
7           <script src="resources/sap-ui-core.js"
8                   id="sap-ui-bootstrap"
9                   data-sap-ui-libs="sap.m"
10                  data-sap-ui-theme="sap_bluecrystal">
11          </script>
12          <!-- only load the mobile lib "sap.m" and the "sap_bluecrystal" theme -->
13      </head>
14  </html>
```

Figure 3.2: Bootstrap syntax

In Figure 3.2 we are loading the OpenUI5 framework from a local web-server, and maintaining configurations under it.

<meta> tag

 <meta> tags in HTML are used to provide information about the data in the document, more specifically for properties of HTML documents, keywords related to it, web services, authors, etc.

Figure 3.2 is explained in the following:

▶ The Source (src) attribute provides a JavaScript resource to find the OpenUI5 core library. From the core library, we get additional resources such as themes (sap_bluecrystal) for page design and UI libraries (sap.m), as specified within their respective attributes.

▶ Because we have loaded all the SAPUI5 components in Eclipse, we specify "resources/sap-ui-core.js". Specify *https://sapui5.hana. ondemand.com/resources/sap-ui-core.js* in src if you want to embed resources online. /resources/ is the reference folder in OpenUI5 installation.

▶ The OpenUI5 libraries are divided into two parts: JavaScript and UI libraries. Instead of using all the resources for UI development, embed only those which are required for development. Correspondingly, we have a variety of JavaScript libraries each having its own use in different cases. The SAPUI5 JavaScript libraries are listed in Table 3.1.

Resource	Description
sap-ui-core.js	This is a default resource with jQuery plug-in and jQuery UI plug-in (jQuery.sap.*). There is a dynamic load to XMLHttpRequests (XHRs).
sap-ui-core-lean.js	This differs to core.js; here, jQuery and only a few SAPUI5 components are loaded immediately, whereas others are loaded during runtime.
sap-ui-core-all.js	This consists of all the resources from the SAPUI5 library. The benefit is that the script avoids having to reload necessary components; however, it increases the initial load time.
sap/ui/core/library-preload.js	This script is similar in structure to the sap-ui-core-all.js, but the components are parsed when required.
sap-ui5.js	This script is a combination of all the JavaScript modules.
sap-ui-custom*.js	For custom developments.

Table 3.1: SAPUI5 JavaScript libraries

▶ Furthermore, we can add multiple libraries in the data-sap-ui-libs attribute, separated by commas.

▶ Within bootstrap, the processes of loading resources can be set to synchronous or asynchronous (loading simultaneously). Enter 'sync' or 'async' in the data-sap-ui-preload attribute.

▶ It is a good practice to define an event Init which fires after completion of loading and initialization. The purpose is to trigger the application logic only when it is required. Figure 3.3 shows the use of the Init function.

```
<html>
  <head>
    <script>
        sap.ui.getCore().attachInit(function (){

            // Your Logic/Controls Code comes here

        });
    </script>
  </head>
</html>
```

Figure 3.3: Use of Init function

3.2   Controls

Controls define the appearance and behavior of UI elements present on the screen. We can either use the native JavaScript or the OpenUI5 library to define controls for an application. The OpenUI5 controls are divided into different UI libraries. To use a control in an application we must embed an appropriate library during bootstrapping.

In Figure 3.4, we have used the control "TextArea", from the "sap.ui.commons" UI library.

```
<script>
        sap.ui.getCore().attachInit(function (){
        new sap.ui.commons.TextArea({
                placeholder: "Hello"
                }).placeAt("content");

    });
</script>
```

Figure 3.4: Controls—TextArea function

▶ The name of the control is "TextArea" and its respective library is prefixed with it. To learn more about this control, you can refer to the demo kit provided by OpenUI5.

▶ Information about libraries, controls and their respective constructor functions, events and methods can be found in API REFERNCE at *https://openui5.hana.ondemand.com/#docs/api/ symbols/sap.ui.html*; or you can access this documentation in Eclipse by using Ctrl + Spacebar key combination.

▶ Figure 3.5 shows the library information for the API reference tab.

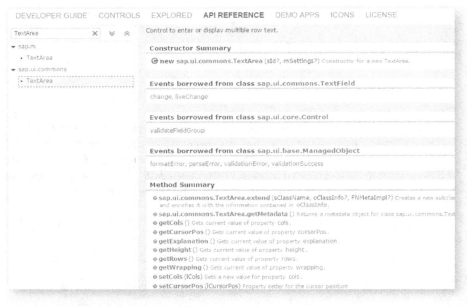

Figure 3.5: Library information—API reference

▶ After creating the control, refer the application content to <body> tag so that it can be displayed. We can achieve this by using the placeAt() function from "sap.ui.core.Control". In our example, "content" is the id of the HTML element.

There are different types of controls in OpenUI5. Let's now have a brief look at each one:

▶ Simple controls—These are the basic controls which, by default, are used in every application design (e.g. buttons, labels, text fields, etc.)

- ▶ Value holders—These controls offer users multiple choices to make or select predefined data maintained by the developer (e.g. ComboBox, DropdownBox, CheckBox and RadioButton-Group).

- ▶ Layouts—These controls are used for setting up page layouts or screen areas such assetting up margins or ruled lines (e.g. MatrixLayout or AbsoluteLayout).

- ▶ Dialogs—These controls act like pop-up windows, or prompting windows, and are very useful for displaying concise data or any sort of system messages (e.g. MessageBox).

- ▶ UX3—These controls include Shell and ThingInspector and are considered to be new-generation controls; for example, we embed the whole application into Shell to make it look intuitive as well as interactive.

- ▶ Complex Controls—These are more flexible and robust when compared to simple controls for displaying content. Combining different, complex controls gives us rich user interfaces.

3.3 Views

Views are important for applying modularization to the program; multiple views can be used on the same logic and any change in logic affects all the views. Having all the U's in one .html file is not recommended because it results in an intricate code setup. Multiple-view types such as XML, HTML, JavaScript and JSON are supported in OpenUI5; the most frequently used is JavaScript.

The syntax for views can be seen in Figure 3.6.

```
sap.ui.jsview(".JS", {
    getControllerName : function() {
        return ".JS";
    },
    createContent : function(oController) {

        });
    }
```

Figure 3.6: Views syntax

▶ `sap.ui.jsview()` indicates the view is in JavaScript format.

▶ `getControllerName()` specifies the controller belonging to this view. If a view doesn't contain a controller, either the implementation fails or a null value is returned

▶ `createContent()` triggers on instantiation of the controller. We construct our UI under this.

3.3.1 XML views

If we select a development paradigm such as XML in Eclipse, we are likely to get an XML view type as shown in Figure 3.7.

```
 1 <core:View xmlns:core="sap.ui.core"
 2            xmlns:mvc="sap.ui.core.mvc"
 3            xmlns="sap.m"
 4            xmlns:html="http://www.w3.org/1999/xhtml">
 5     <Page title="Title">
 6         <content>
 7             <!-- Controls are defined here for the Page-->
 8         </content>
 9     </Page>
10 </core:View>
```

Figure 3.7: XML views syntax

A new XML file with *.view.xml* extension is created. In our XML file, "view" is considered to be the root node. XML is written in hierarchical format and uses namespaces to avoid element name conflicts.

From our example library, `sap.m` holds all the major UI controls and `sap.ui.core.mvc` holds all OpenUI5 views and MVC contents with an alias **mvc**. <Page> is a UI control in the sap.m library.

3.3.2 JSON views

JavaScript Object Notation (JSON) is one of the many views supported by OpenUI5. The view file name ends with *.view.json*. JSON is easier to understand, consumes less space and is faster than XML. JSON is written in hierarchical format as with XML and supports the use of arrays.

The drawback of JSON is that it becomes confusing for beginners due to the use of multiple parentheses.

```
1  {
2      "Type":"sap.ui.core.mvc.JSONView",
3      "controllerName":"example.view",
4      "content": [{
5          "Type":"sap.m.Page",
6          "title":"Title",
7          "content":[
8
9          ]
10     }]
11 }
```

Figure 3.8: JSON view syntax

In JSON, data is represented in name-value pairs; *name* consists of all properties of a control and *value* holds a control's corresponding value. Both name and value are separated by a semi-colon and are written within double quotation marks. Refer to Figure 3.8 for JSON view syntax.

3.3.3 HTML views

The Hypertext Markup Language (HTML) view is a pre-defined view supported by OpenUI5. This view file name ends with *.view.html*. HTML views follow declarative programming; i.e. UI is considered an element in an HTML document. A good example of the HTML views syntax is shown in Figure 3.9.

```
1  <template data-controller-name="example.View">
2      <div data-sap-ui-type="sap.m.Page" data-title="Title">
3          <div data-sap-ui-aggregation="content">
4
5          </div>
6      </div>
7  </template>
```

Figure 3.9: HTML views syntax

3.4 Fragments and components

Fragments are reusable UI parts similar to views, but they don't require a controller. The use of fragments is to provide modularization to the program; for example, instead of using the same UI controls in different views, we can create a fragment consisting of reusable UI controls. Fragments are independent and can be used without MVC.

To provide flexibility to developers, OpenUI5 supports three different fragments: XML, HTML and JS. All file names ending with .fragments are defined fragments.

► HTML fragments, compared to HTML views, are declared without <template> tag.

► Similarly, XML fragments are created without the <View> tag as in root element.

► JS fragments have a fragment name and createContent() function. Compared to JS views, it does not have getController-Name().

Components, like fragments, are used for applying modularization in a program. Components can be created by different developers at different locations and can be used in various applications. OpenUI5 supports two types of components:

► UI Components—these extend functionality and rendering possibilities for components.

► Faceless Components—these don't contain any UI.

3.5 Controllers

We create UI in views and all the events for that UI are handled under the controller section. *Controllers* are the most important part of OpenUI5; this is where all the application logics are written. Furthermore, a controller handles how an application behaves before, at the start, and after rendering, as well as on exiting a page. All the files in controller are suffixed by *.controller.js* namespace.

- ► Controllers consist of four pre-defined functions, also known as life cycle hooks:

  1. `onInit()`—triggers during installation

  2. `onBeforeRendering()`—triggers before rendering the page

  3. `onAfterRendering()`—triggers after rendering the page

  4. `onExit()`—triggers when closing the page

- ► Along with life cycle hooks, additional event handlers and functionality can be managed by the controller.

- ► Where one view exists for every one controller, the controller carries the same name as the related view.

- ► Creating a controller for every view is recommended, but is not necessary; we can replace a view for its corresponding controller at any time.

3.6 Data binding

Data binding is used to bind controls to application data (model), so that any changes in the application data automatically update the controls on the front-end (e.g. data displayed in the form of tables, lists, etc). Correspondingly, if using a data binding model, data can be updated or changed using UI controls (e.g. filling out a simple form).

Data can be updated synchronously and asynchronously between model and controls, depending on the binding mode. Binding modes define how the data is bound. OpenUI5 supports three modes of binding:

One-way Binding is from model to view. Any update in model changes the data in view, any number of times.

Two-way Binding is from model to view and also from view to model; it changes if either of them updates the other.

One-time Binding is similar to one-way binding but updates data only once.

Now we know the binding modes, let's look at how various OpenUI5 models support them. OpenUI5 provides three data binding patterns— JSON, XML and OData. Each pattern has its own service or functionality.

Data binding for models can be viewed in Table 3.2.

Model	Default mode	One-time	One-way	Two-way
JSON	two-way	x	x	x
XML	two-way	x	x	x
OData	one-way	x	x	x
Resource	one-time	x	-	-

Table 3.2: Data binding for Models

3.6.1 Types of binding

Property binding

Binding properties of control to a model can be done through property binding. There are different steps to bind properties to control:

▶ within parenthesis of the constructor, or

▶ through the bindProperty() method

After binding, data updates in both the model and in the control synchronously or asynchronously depending upon the binding mode. Model instances always use their default binding mode; we can change binding by using the mode attribute. Figure 3.10 demonstrates property binding. In this example, data binding is done in JS syntax.

We can use either the "value" or "path" attribute for binding data; the difference between them is the use of parentheses. In our example, the Input field shows the price value (i.e. 20$).

```
//JSON Data
{
"Pizza" :{
"Bread" : "Wheat",
"Cheese" : "American",
"Toppings": "Pepperoni",
"Price" : "20$"
}
}

//Property Binding JS
var Input = new sap.m.Input({
    value: "{/Pizza/Price}",
    mode: 'sap.ui.model.BindingMode.OneWay'
});
(OR)
// Using JS Object for defining path.
var Input = new sap.m.Input({
    path: "/Pizza/Price",
    mode: 'sap.ui.model.BindingMode.OneWay' '
});
```

Figure 3.10: Types of binding—property binding

Similarly, data binding is also possible in XML format, as shown in the example in Figure 3.11.

```
//Property Binding XML
<mvc:View
xmlns="sap.m"
xmlns:mvc="sap.ui.core.mvc">
    <Input
        value: "{/Pizza/Price}",
        mode: 'sap.ui.model.BindingMode.OneWay'
    />
</mvc:View>
```

Figure 3.11: Types of binding—property binding XML

Aggregation binding

Binding a collection of values or data to a specific control can be achieved through aggregation binding. This can be done in two ways:

► using the bindAggregation() method, or

► defining aggregation binding within constructor parentheses

The control acts like a container and holds the template of the data; for example, JSON data is passed into a template and then the template data is bound to a control (table, list, etc.). Refer to Figure 3.12 for aggregation binding; syntax for aggregation binding using parentheses.

```
var oTemplate = new sap.ui.core.ListItem({text: "{aggProperty}"});
var oControl = new sap.ui.commons.ComboBox({
        items:{path:"modelAggregate", template: oTemplate}
        });
              (OR)
    oControl.bindAggregation("items","modelAggregate",oTemplate);
```

Figure 3.12: Types of binding—aggregation binding

```
<script>
    var jData = {
            "fieldname": "Groceries",
            "products": [{"text":"Milk"},
                        {"text":"Bread"},
                        {"text": "Cheese"}]
            };
    var oModel = new sap.ui.model.json.JSONModel();
        oModel.setData(jData);

    var oTemplate = new sap.ui.core.ListItem({text: "{text}"});

    var oComboBox = new sap.ui.commons.ComboBox({
        items:{path:"/products", template: oTemplate}
    });
        oComboBox.bindValue("/fieldname");
        oComboBox.setModel(oModel);
        oComboBox.placeAt("content");
</script>
```

Figure 3.13: Aggregation binding sample

Figure 3.13 shows an example of aggregation binding. We have used the *ListItem* control which acts like a template.

The bindValue() method shows the text on the control.

The output for aggregation binding can be seen in Figure 3.14.

Figure 3.14: Aggregation binding output

Element binding

Binding elements to a specific object in a model can be done through element binding; this yields a context for relative binding to a control. A parent-child or master-detail relationship is necessary for this type of binding; for example, displaying a list of item level data (child) on selecting a specific header level value (parent).

To bind an element, we use the bindElement() method on a control.

Having covered the binding modes and types, we now need to look at how different model patterns support them. OpenUI5 provides three data-binding patterns: JSON, XML and OData. Each pattern has its own service or functionality.

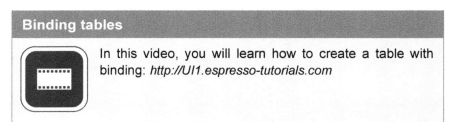

Binding tables

In this video, you will learn how to create a table with binding: *http://UI1.espresso-tutorials.com*

3.7   Models

3.7.1   JSON model

The *JSON model* is a client-side model; i.e. all the operations on data are performed on the client side. The JSON model is mainly used for small data content and doesn't involve any operation on the server side. Nonetheless, it supports a two-way binding model.

Syntax to initiate a JSON model can be seen in Figure 3.15.

```
//Creating Instance of JSON Model
var oModel = new sap.ui.model.json.JSONModel();
```

Figure 3.15: JSON model initiate syntax

After creating the instance, we need to load data into the model by using the *loadData()* method. We can either specify a URL here (if we want to load from the server side) or a file path, as can be seen in Figure 3.16.

```
//Loading data into the model through URL
oModel.loadData("<URL>")

//Loading data by specifying path
oModel.loadData("filename.json");
```

Figure 3.16: JSON model data load

Alternatively, data can be presented by writing down the content inside a *.setData()* method, as seen in Figure 3.17.

```
//Loading data into Model
oModel.setData({
Name: "Harry",
Age: 23
});
```

Figure 3.17: JSON model data load into model

3.7.2   XML model

Like JSON, the *XML model* is a client-side model—supporting two-way binding—and doesn't involve any data operations on the server side. The XML model uses an XML data file (i.e. it has *.xml* as an extension). Like JSON, XML documents cannot be embedded inside JavaScript, so for that we need to refer to an XML document name inside the *.setData()* method. The syntax to instantiate an XML model, followed by the *.loadData()* and *.setData()* method, is shown in Figure 3.18 below.

```
//Creating Instance of XML Model
//loading data into it.
var oModel = new sap.ui.model.xml.XMLModel();
oModel.loadData("<URL>/filename");
            (OR)
oModel.setData(XML filename);
```

Figure 3.18: XML model syntax

3.7.3   OData Model

The *Open Data Protocol (OData)* model is a server-side model; i.e. all the client request operations are done on the server and sent back to the client as a response. OData supports one-way binding.

Refer to Figure 3.19 for the syntax to create a model instance using OData (a URL is required).

```
//OData Instance Model
var oModel = new sap.ui.core.model.odata.ODataModel("<URL>");
            (OR)
//Latest OData Instance Model
var oModel = new sap.ui.core.model.odata.v2.ODataModel("<URl>")
```

Figure 3.19: OData syntax

3.8   Navigation and routing

Navigation in OpenUI5 is required in the following cases:

▶   to enable moving back and forth between the pages, especially for mobile devices without a physical back button

▶   to provide a bookmark or deep-link functionality in applications, so that users can resume their work where they last left off

Navigation in OpenUI5 for a single-page application is hash-based; i.e. instead of using URL or server path parameters, hash is used. The server sends only one resource on request and the rest of the additional resources are dynamically loaded using client-side logic.

URL in hash-tag navigation is like *http://<host-name>/<path>/#/additional /info*. Router is a UI5 API that is available in the *sap.m.routing.Router* library. This initiates navigation within an application by adding a hash value. Using a router makes the navigation efficient and provides a URL for a single page in an application. This allows the user to bookmark a page and use it later. The three properties that are used to configure routing are:

▶   config—which is a global configuration

▶   routes—where you define your route to navigate to your target

▶   targets—which define views; each target has a unique key.

Application process navigation

 In this video, you will learn how to navigate through the application process: *http://UI2.espresso-tutorials.com*

3.9   Simple types in OpenUI5

Objects in a model can be assigned data types during binding in order to converting values into a desired format (e.g. decimal points in a price or any required date format).

The following are the data types supported in OpenUI5 with data binding:

▶ For **Integers** the value in the model should be a number and is represented by type `sap.ui.model.type.Integer`. This type allows conversion into float and string values.

Syntax for initialization of this type and `sap.ui.core.format.NumberFormat` class options for formatting are shown in Figure 3.20.

```
var typeInt = sap.ui.model.type.Integer({
        minIntergerDigits: 1,  //Minimum number of integer digits
        maxIntergerDigits: 99, //Maximum number of integer digits
        minFractionDigits: 0, //Minimum number of fractional digits
        maxFractionDigits: 0, //Maximum number of fractional digits
        groupingEnabled: false, // Enable Grouping
        groupingSeparator: ",", //Grouping Seperator used
        decimalSeparator: "."//Decimal Seperator used
});
```

Figure 3.20: Simple type syntax.

▶ **Floating type numbers are represented by** `sap.ui.model.format.Float`; the value in the model should represent a float value and, depending on the binding property, conversion into integer and string is possible. It uses the same class as integers (i.e. `sap.ui.core.format.NumberFormat`).

▶ **Strings** are represented by `sap.ui.model.type.String`. The value in the model must be a string and, depending on the binding property, it is converted into integer and floating point.

▶ **Booleans** values are either true or false. Here, we initialize Boolean values with `sap.ui.model.type.Boolean()`, where 'X' represents true and " " (empty space within quotation marks) represents false.

▶ To represent **Date** without time we have `sap.ui.model.type.Date`. This type is used to transform a model value into a date string. Similarly, we have `sap.ui.model.type.DateTime` to convert the model data into a date + time string.

▶ Refer to Figure 3.21 for an example of the simple type.

```
onInit: function() {
    var oModel = new sap.ui.model.json.JSONModel({
        date1 : "2016-02-11",   //Date Format
        time1 : "04.43.23"      //Time Format
    });
    this.getView().setModel(oModel);
}


<Text
    text="{
            path: '/date1',
            type: 'sap.ui.model.type.Date',
            formatOptions: { source: {pattern: 'yyyy-MM-dd'},
                            pattern: 'yyyy/MM/dd'
                         }
        }"
/>
```

Figure 3.21: Simple type example code

▶ For **Time** we use `sap.ui.model.type.Time` for conversion of data in a time string.

▶ Figure 3.22 gives an example of simple type time

```
<Text
    text="{
            path: '/time1',
            type: 'sap.ui.model.type.Time',
            formatOptions: { source: {pattern: 'HH.mm.ss'},
                            pattern: 'HH:mm:ssss'
                         }
        }"
/>
```

Figure 3.22: Example of simple type in OpenUI5—time

2016/02/11 04:43:0023

Figure 3.23: Example of simple type in OpenUI5—time, output

Date and time patterns must be defined using Local Data Markup Language (LDML) format notation or styles, using predefined formats such as short, medium, long and full.

Data typing without binding is considered a formatter class. OpenUI5 provides two formatter classes:

- ▶ To get a JS-based date object from a string, we use formatter class `sap.ui.core.format.DateFormat`.

- ▶ Similarly, to get a JS-based number from a string, formatter class `sap.ui.core.format.NumberFormat` is used.

3.10 Internationalization and localization

A separate file is created for storing all hard-coded text. This enables text to be translated into any language. This process is called internationalization, or i18n.

The file name ends with *.properties*, where the text is written in the format of name-value pairs. Each separate file should be created for its respective language. It is recommended to follow specific naming conventions when naming the file; for example, the internationalization file for the English language would be *i18n_en.properties*, or *i18n_fr.properties* for French.

Example:

A file i18n_de is created under a folder i18n which has a name- value pair. All files should be stored with the same extension "*.properties*", preferably with a language suffix such as "_de", as seen in Figure 3.24.

45

Figure 3.24: Example for internationalization

You create an app and place a page in it, as shown in Figure 3.25.

```
<script src="resources/sap-ui-core.js"
        id="sap-ui-bootstrap"
        data-sap-ui-libs="sap.m"
        data-sap-ui-theme="sap_bluecrystal"
        data-sap-ui-resourceroots='{ "translation": "./" }'>
</script>
<!-- only load the mobile lib "sap.m" and the "sap_bluecrystal" theme -->

<script>
        sap.ui.localResources("translation");
        var app = new sap.m.App({initialPage:"idview11"});
        var page = sap.ui.view({id:"idview11", viewName:"translation.view1", type:sap.ui.
        app.addPage(page);
        app.placeAt("content");
</script>
```

Figure 3.25: Bootstrapping in internationalization

The resource model holds the resource files which include the localized texts. This localized text can be used as a model. Next, we initiate the resource with a bundleName and then bind the data as usual. This code syntax is shown in Figure 3.26 and the output can be seen in Figure 3.27.

46

```
onInit: function() {
    var oResourceModel = new sap.ui.model.resource.ResourceModel({
        bundleName : "translation.i18n.i18n_de"
    });
    sap.ui.getCore().setModel(oResourceModel, "i18n");
},
```

Figure 3.26: Code example

Title

Das ist deutsch

Figure 3.27: Internationalization output

47

4 Controls

Controls define the appearance and behavior of UI elements present on the screen. We can either use the native JavaScript or OpenUI5 library to define controls for an application. The OpenUI5 controls are divided into different UI libraries and to use a control in an application we have to embed an appropriate library during bootstrapping.

4.1 Layouts

OpenUI5 uses layouts functionality for arranging various UI controls on the screen. This involves sizing, spacing and proper placement of controls in order to make it aesthetically pleasing. We have various layout supports under OpenUI5: absolute, vertical, horizontal, matrix, border, form, grid, responsive layout, simple form, panel layout, splitter control and tabstrip.

4.1.1 Absolute layout

An absolute layout places the controls just like a CSS "absolute" statement. We use this layout if we know that our screen area is fixed, otherwise, on resizing the screen, controls may overlap.

An instance of this layout is created with:
```
sap.ui.commons.layout.AbsoluteLayout.
```

Figure 4.1 shows two controls overlapping each other in absolute layout. The position of the controls can be changed by using position properties (i.e. top, left, etc.).

```
<script>
var oAbsoluteLayout = new sap.ui.commons.layout.AbsoluteLayout({
    width: "300px",
    height: "300px"
});
oAbsoluteLayout.placeAt("content")
var oTextArea = new sap.ui.commons.TextArea();
oAbsoluteLayout.addContent(oTextArea);
var oButton2 = new sap.ui.commons.Button({text: "Button 3"});
oAbsoluteLayout.addContent(oButton2);
</script>
```

Figure 4.1: Layout—absolute layout example

Figure 4.2: Layout—absolute layout example, output

4.1.2   Vertical and horizontal layout

A vertical layout aligns all controls vertically; i.e. one below the other. The controls are arranged in one column. The instance for vertical layout is defined with `sap.ui.commons.layout.VerticalLayout`, as shown in Figure 4.3.

```
var oVerticalLayout = new sap.ui.commons.layout.VerticalLayout();
oVerticalLayout.placeAt("content");
var oTextField = new sap.ui.commons.TextField({placeholder:"Vertical 1"});
oVerticalLayout.addContent(oTextField);
var oTextField1 = new sap.ui.commons.TextField({placeholder:"Vertical 2"});
oVerticalLayout.addContent(oTextField1);
var oHorizontalLayout = new sap.ui.layout.HorizontalLayout();
oVerticalLayout.addContent(oHorizontalLayout);
var oTextField2 = new sap.ui.commons.TextField({placeholder:"Horizontal 3"});
oHorizontalLayout.addContent(oTextField2);
var oTextField3 = new sap.ui.commons.TextField({placeholder:"Horizontal 4"});
oHorizontalLayout.addContent(oTextField3);
```

Figure 4.3: Horizontal and vertical layout example

50

Figure 4.4: Horizontal and vertical layout example, output

4.1.3   Matrix layout

A matrix layout is used to arrange multiple controls in a grid structure. For this layout, we can set the cell size to constant with the setting attribute "layoutFixed=true", or set it to variable with the setting "layoutFixed=false".

```
//Instance of Matrix Layout
var oMatrixLayout = new sap.ui.commons.layout.MatrixLayout({
    width: "350px",
    visible: true,
    layoutFixed: true,
    columns: 2
});
oMatrixLayout.placeAt("content");
var oMatrixLayoutCell = new sap.ui.commons.layout.MatrixLayoutCell({
    backgroundDesign: "Border",
    colSpan: 1, rowSpan: 1
});
var oTextView2 = new sap.ui.commons.TextView({text: "Matrix Layout R1",design: "H3"});
oMatrixLayoutCell.addContent(oTextView2);
oMatrixLayout.createRow(oMatrixLayoutCell);

var oLabel = new sap.ui.commons.Label({text: "R2-C1"});
var oTextView = new sap.ui.commons.TextView({text: "R2-C2"});
oMatrixLayout.createRow(oLabel, oTextView);

var oLabel1 = new sap.ui.commons.Label({text: "R3-C1"});
var oTextView1 = new sap.ui.commons.TextView({text: "R3-C2"});
oMatrixLayout.createRow(oLabel1, oTextView1);
```

Figure 4.5: Matrix layout example

Matrix Layout R1-C1	
R2-C1	R2-C2
R3-C1	R3-C2

Figure 4.6: Matrix layout example, output

In Figure 4.5 above, we entered the number of columns as 2; it is good practice to enter the number of columns because it reduces the load on the system. Every control or set of controls must be placed inside a row by using *createRow()*. An additional control, matrixLayoutCell, is used to create separate cells (blocks) for the inner structure of the matrix layout.

4.1.4 Border layout

A border layout is used to divide a screen into 5 sub-areas—top and bottom, begin, center and end. Within each area we can embed one or more controls and optionally set different layouts for them. The instance of this layout is created using `sap.ui.commons.layout.BorderLayout`, as shown in Figure 4.7.

```
var oBorderLayout =  new sap.ui.commons.layout.BorderLayout({
    width: "800px",
    height: "300px",
    top: new sap.ui.commons.layout.BorderLayoutArea({
        size: "30%",
        contentAlign: "center",
        content: [new sap.ui.commons.TextField({placeholder:"Top"})]
    }),
    begin: new sap.ui.commons.layout.BorderLayoutArea({
        contentAlign: "center", size: "30%",
        content: [new sap.ui.commons.TextField({placeholder:"Begin"})]
    }),
    center: new sap.ui.commons.layout.BorderLayoutArea({
        contentAlign: "center", width: "5px", height: "5px",
        content: [new sap.ui.commons.TextField({placeholder:"Center"})]
    }),
    end: new sap.ui.commons.layout.BorderLayoutArea({
        contentAlign: "center", size:"30%",
        content: [new sap.ui.commons.TextField({placeholder:"End"})]
    }),
    bottom: new sap.ui.commons.layout.BorderLayoutArea({
        contentAlign: "center",
        content: [new sap.ui.commons.TextField({placeholder:"Bottom"})]
    })
});
oBorderLayout.placeAt("content");
```

Figure 4.7: Border layout example

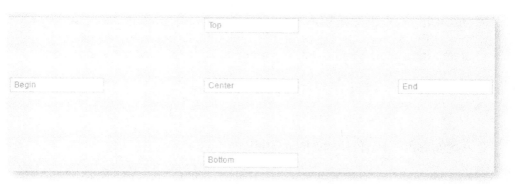

Figure 4.8: Border layout example, output

To represent each part of a page, we use:
`sap.ui.commons.layout.BorderLayoutArea` or
`sap.ui.commons.layout.BorderLayoutAreaTypes` followed by
position (.bottom, .top, .end, etc.)

4.1.5 Form Layout

Forms are placed on web pages to enable users to enter data to be processed. OpenUI5 has different controls for creating a form: Form, FormContainer and FormElement.

The *Form* is used to hold all the content of the form. Inside the form, *FormContainer* is used to create separate blocks, which helps in categorizing form fields. Finally, within the FormContainer, we can use one or more *FormElements* where single or multiple UI controls are placed.

The instance of FormElement is created using:

`sap.ui.commons.form.FormElement()`, for FormContainer using
`sap.ui.commons.form.FormContainer()`.

Additionally, a form can be set into different layouts, which causes its visualization and interaction to change. Layouts are also set to define the way to render the Form, which is achieved with the setting "LayoutData". There are 3 layouts supported by forms: GridLayout, ResponsiveLayout and ResponsiveGridLayout.

OpenUI5 provides *SimpleForm*, a better and simpler control for creating forms. Form, FormContainer and FormElements are automatically generated for a SimpleForm; only the required controls need to be provided. The instance for creating a SimpleForm is `sap.ui.layout.form.SimpleForm` or `sap.ui.commons.form.SimpleForm`.

A SimpleForm with responsiveGridLayout

As we see in our example in Figure 4.9, a control type "Title" (`sap.ui.core.Title`) creates a FormContainer and underneath it, the controls (labels and text fields) represent the FormElements. This form is created using ResponsiveGridLayout.

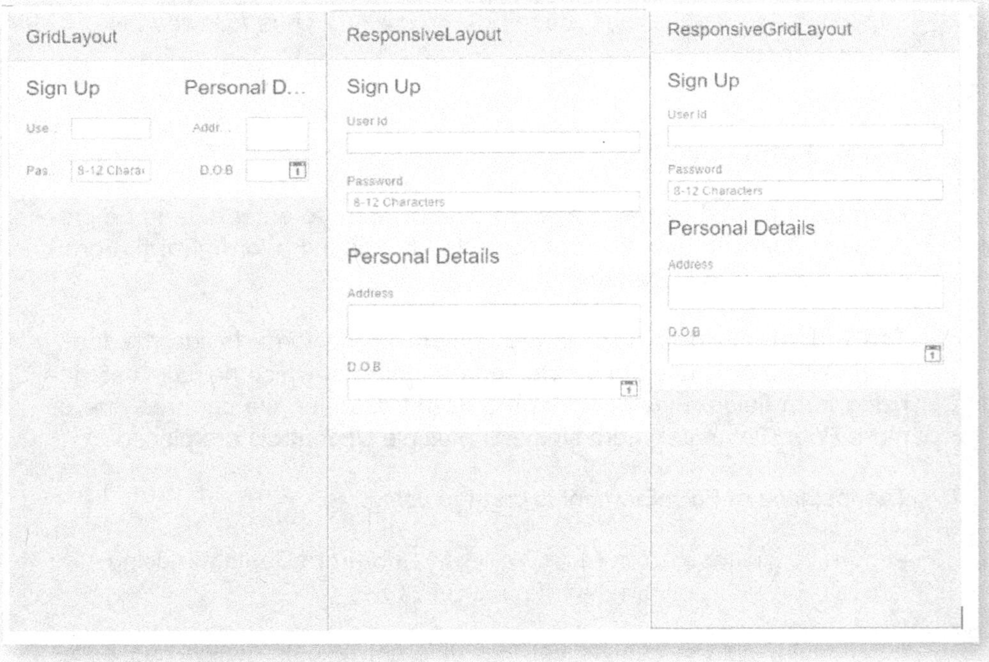

Figure 4.9: Layout—responsive grid layout

Figure 4.9 shows a SimpleForm rendering in different layouts after changing the screen area.

4.1.6 Panel layout

A panel is a UI control available in sap.m and the sap.ui.commons library; it consists of a header and a body area. The header area can hold title/text, buttons and icons, with additional functionality to expand or collapse. However, the body area holds the rest of the controls in the page or the whole page itself.

In Figure 4.10, we have embedded the previous SimpleForm into the Panel. The instance of Panel is created using sap.ui.commons.Panel.

```
<script>
var oPanel = new sap.ui.commons.Panel({
    width:"100%",
    showCollapseIcon:true,
    title: new sap.ui.commons.Title({
        icon:"sap-icon://activity-individual",
        level:"H1",
        text:"Panel"})
});
oPanel.placeAt("content");
var oSimpleForm = new sap.ui.layout.form.SimpleForm({
    breakpointL:1024,      <!--Additional Properties of setting SimpleForm-->
    breakpointM:600,
    columnsL:2,
    columnsM:1,
    labelMinWidth:192,
    labelSpanL:4,
    labelSpanM:2,
    labelSpanS:12,
    "layout":"ResponsiveGridLayout",
    maxContainerCols:2,
    title:"SimpleForm",
    });
oPanel.addContent(oSimpleForm);
// ..... Code for SimpleForm continues
</script>
```

Figure 4.10: Panel layout example

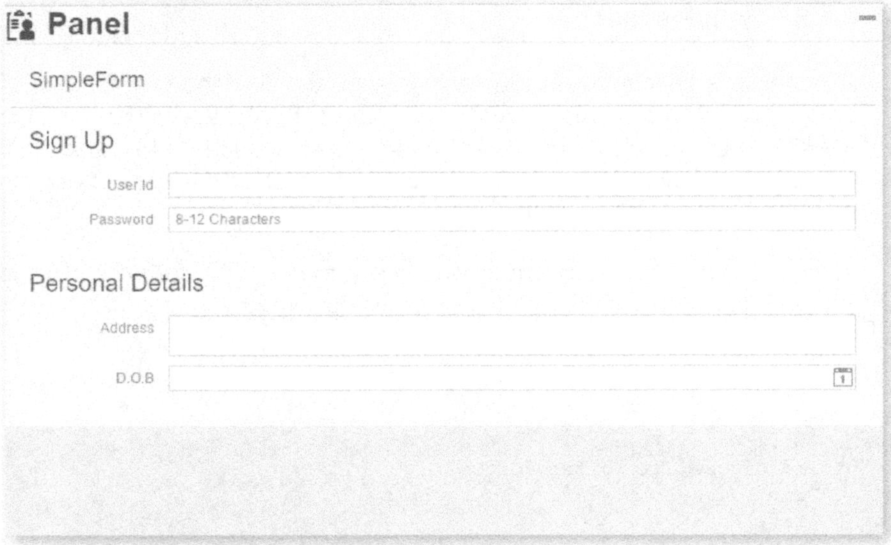

Figure 4.11: Panel layout example, output

In the header area in Figure 4.10 we have used the icon, text and expand/collapse (far right in the panel) buttons. The body area holds the rest of the content. We can create multiple panels within the page, or side by side, using a matrix layout.

4.1.7 Splitter control

A splitter control divides the screen into two different sections, called panes. The panes on each side hold areas which can be modified by dragging the separator. The areas can be separated horizontally or vertically by using the splitterOrientation attribute.

An instance of Splitter is created with `sap.ui.commons.Splitter`, as shown in Figure 4.12.

```
<script>
var oSplitter = new sap.ui.commons.Splitter({
    height:"500px",
    splitterBarVisible:true,
    splitterOrientation:"Horizontal",
    splitterPosition:"50%",
    width:"400px"});
oSplitter.placeAt("content");
 var oTextView = new sap.ui.commons.TextView({text:"First Pane Content"});
oSplitter.addFirstPaneContent(oTextView);
 var oTextView1 = new sap.ui.commons.TextView({text:"Second Pane Content"});
oSplitter.addSecondPaneContent(oTextView1);
var oSplitter1 = new sap.ui.commons.Splitter({
    height:"500px",
    splitterBarVisible:true,
    splitterOrientation:"Vertical",
    splitterPosition:"20%",
    width:"400px"});
oSplitter.addSecondPaneContent(oSplitter1);
var oButton = new sap.ui.commons.Button({text:"Button"});
oSplitter1.addFirstPaneContent(oButton);
var oButton1 = new sap.ui.commons.Button({text:"Button 2"});
oSplitter1.addSecondPaneContent(oButton1);
</script>
```

Figure 4.12: Layout—splitter control

First Pane Content

Second Pane Content

Button   Button 2   ∧

Figure 4.13: Layout—splitter control

Every Splitter control has 2 panes; we specify the first and second pane with the attributes "addFirstPaneContent" and "addSecondPaneContent". Always make sure to enter the height of the splitter control or else the height will be calculated by the height of its controls.

4.1.8   Tabstrip control

A tabstrip control is a container which enables us to create tabs on the page. Every tab holds a set of controls and allows users to switch between them according to their needs.

An instance of a TabStrip is created with `sap.ui.commons.TabStrip`. A tabstrip generally holds a set of tabs. An instance of a tab is created with `sap.ui.commons.Tab` and is added into TabStrip with the addContent attribute. Figure 4.14 provides a simple example of a tabstrip control layout.

```
<script>
var oTabStrip = new sap.ui.commons.TabStrip();
oTabStrip.placeAt("content");
 var oTab = new sap.ui.commons.Tab({
    title: new sap.ui.core.Title({emphasized:true,text:"Tab 1"})
 });
oTabStrip.addTab(oTab);
 var oTab1 = new sap.ui.commons.Tab({
        title: new sap.ui.core.Title({text:"Tab 2"})
 });
oTabStrip.addTab(oTab1);
 var oTabStrip1 = new sap.ui.commons.TabStrip();
oTab1.addContent(oTabStrip1);
 var oTab2 = new sap.ui.commons.Tab({
    closable:true,
    title: new sap.ui.core.Title({text:"Nested Tab 1"})
 });
oTabStrip1.addTab(oTab2);
 var oTextView = new sap.ui.commons.TextView({text:"Contents of this Nested tab"});
oTab2.addContent(oTextView);
 var oTab3 = new sap.ui.commons.Tab({
    enabled:false,
    closable:true,
    title: new sap.ui.core.Title({text:"Nested Tab 2"})
 });
oTabStrip1.addTab(oTab3);
</script>
```

Figure 4.14: Layout—tabstrip control

Figure 4.15: Layout—tabstrip control, output

A tab can be identified by a label/text or icon. Nesting of tabs is possible; i.e. one tab embedded within the other—for this scenario we need to create two tabstrips.

4.2 Dialogs and message box

4.2.1 Dialog

Dialog controls are limited or fixed-size windows that appear on front of the application page only after user interaction; these are also known as pop-up windows or dialog windows. Dialog Boxes display brief information and require some sort of action to return to the parent window.

Within dialog boxes, buttons are added using `addbutton()` and are assigned press events. Any number of buttons can be added to the dialog box.

```
<script>
var oButton = new sap.ui.commons.Button({text:"Button",press:function(){oDialog.open();}});
   oButton.placeAt("content");
var oDialog = new sap.ui.commons.Dialog({
      title: "Dialog Box",
      height: "300px",
      width: "400px"
      });
   oDialog.placeAt("content");
var odiaButton = new sap.ui.commons.Button({text:"Okay", press:function(){oDialog.close();}})
oDialog.addButton(odiaButton);
var oModel = new sap.ui.model.json.JSONModel();
oModel.loadData("json/week.json")
var oTable = new sap.ui.table.Table({
         title: "Meal Plan",
         visibleRowCount: 7,
      });
      oDialog.addContent(oTable);
      oTable.addColumn(new sap.ui.table.Column({
      label: new sap.ui.commons.Label({text: "DAY"}),
      template: new sap.ui.commons.TextView().bindProperty("text", "we_day"),
      width: "150px"
      }));
      oTable.addColumn(new sap.ui.table.Column({
      label: new sap.ui.commons.Label({ text: "Comments"}),
      template: new sap.ui.commons.TextView().bindProperty( "text", "we_comment"),
      width: "150px"
      }));
      oTable.setModel(oModel);
      oTable.bindRows("/week");
</script>
```

Figure 4.16: Dialog syntax and output

Figure 4.17: Dialog syntax and output, output

60

In our example in Figure 4.16, we have created a button on a page and attached `oDialog.open()` (..open() is for opening a dialog box) and inside the dialog box is a button with `oDialog.close()` (..close() is for closing the dialog box). Correspondingly, a table is attached inside the box which displays some brief information.

4.2.2 Message box

Message boxes are used to display messages for processed transactions after user interactions. Message boxes are configured with native JS method parameters such as `alert()`, `confirm()` and `show()`. The only difference is that message boxes are event driven so when they are called, a dialog control is created and rendered.

We use `alert()` to display small messages or warnings with an OK button. Alert boxes don't have headers and multiple buttons.

To use alert MessageBox, enter `MessageBox.alert("<some message>")`.

Figure 4.18 shows an example of message box syntax and output.

```
<script>
    var oButton = new sap.ui.commons.Button({
        text:"Alert Button",
        press: function(){
            var oMessageBox = new sap.ui.commons.MessageBox.alert("This is Alert Box");
            }
    });
    oButton.placeAt("content");
</script>
```

Figure 4.18: Message box syntax

Figure 4.19: Message box output

If we use `confirm()`, the user receives a small message along with an option to proceed or not, and a question mark icon. The syntax for using the `confirm()` method is: `sap.ui.commons.MessageBox.confirm(sMessage, fncallBack, sTitle)`.

Figure 4.20 shows an example of a confirmation message box.

```
<script>
    var oButton = new sap.ui.commons.Button({
        text:"Confirm Button",
        press: function(){
            var oMessageBox = new sap.ui.commons.MessageBox.confirm("This is a confirmation box", function(){}, "Title");
        }
    });
    oButton.placeAt("content");
</script>
```

Figure 4.20: Confirmation message box

Figure 4.21: Confirmation message box, output

The syntax for using `show()` is: `sap.ui.commons.MessageBox.show (sMessage, oIcon, sTitle, vActions, fnCallBack, oDefaultAction)`.

Refer to Figure 4.22 for an example of a confirmation message box—"proceed" type.

```
<script>
    var oButton = new sap.ui.commons.Button({
        text:"Confirm Button",
        press: function(){
            var oMessageBox = new sap.ui.commons.MessageBox.show("Do you want to proceed", "WARNING","MessageBox
            ["YES","NO","IGNORE"],function(){},"");
        }
    });
    oButton.placeAt("content");
</script>
```

Figure 4.22: Confirmation message box—proceed type

Figure 4.23: Confirmation message box—proceed type, output

4.3   Control types

4.3.1   Simple type

Simple controls, code (with important properties) and output

The explanations below give an overview of simple controls with respect to their code. We also list important properties and, in most cases, show the output.

Button

(sap.m, sap.ui.commons)

▶   for users to trigger some actionS

```
sap.ui.commons.Button({
    height: "50px",
    style: "Reject",
    styled: true,
    text: "Button",
    width: "100px",
    icon: "sap-icon://home"
});
```

Color Picker

(sap.ui.commons)

► a control to choose color

► colors are defined using HEX, RGB or HSV values.

```
sap.ui.commons.ColorPicker();
```

Formatted Text

(sap.ui.commons)

► limit the usage of HTML tags

```
sap.ui.commons.FormattedTextView({
    htmlText: "This is formatted Text
});
```

Icon

(sap.ui.commons, sap.m.MessageBox, sap.ui.core)

► embedded image, supports various effects of CSS

```
sap.ui.core.Icon({
    color: "Blue",
    decorative: true,
    height: "90px",
    hoverColor: "red",
    src: "sap-icon://home",
    width: "80px"
});
```

Image

(sap.m,sap.ui.commons)

► loading of images is possible on local and remote servers.

```
sap.ui.commons.Image({
    src: "http://........",
    height: "100px",
    width: "100px"
});
```

Label

(sap.ui.commons, sap.m, sap.ui.core)

► provides labels to other controls

```
sap.ui.commons.Label({
    design: "Bold",
    text: "LABEL",
    textAlign: "Begin"
});
```

LABEL

Link

(sap.m, sap.ui.commons)

► navigation to web-pages or other applications

TextView

(sap.ui.commons)

▶ headings and paragraphs

```
sap.ui.commons.TextView({
        design: "H2"
        text: "Text View"
   });
```

ToggleButton

(sap.m, sap.ui.commons)

▶ two states—pressed and normal

```
sap.ui.commons.ToggleButton({
        style: "Default",
        text: "Toggle Button"
        });
```

BusyIndicator

(sap.m, sap.ui.core)

▶ similar to loading indicator

```
sap.m.BusyIndicator({
        design: "dark"
     });
```

StandardTile

(sap.m)

▶ similar to button, used mostly for dashboard design

```
sap.m.StandardTile({
    info: "Standard Tile",
    number: "11",
    numberUnit: "pieces",
    title: "Tile"
});
```

11
PIECES

Tile

Standard Tile

ObjectNumber

(sap.m)

▶ displays number along with unit.

```
sap.m.ObjectNumber({
    emphasized: true,
    number: 100,
    numberUnit: "USD",
    state: "None"
});
```

100 USD

ObjectStatus

(sap.m)

▶ shows status either through icon or text

```
sap.m.ObjectStatus({
    icon: "sap-icon://accept",
    state: "Success",
    title :"Object Status"
    });
```

PullToRefresh

(sap.m)

▶ in touch devices, occurs when user pulls down a list (optional to hide)

```
sap.m.PullToRefresh({
    showIcon: false,
    iconDensityAware: true
    });
```

⟳ REFRESH

4.3.2   Value holders

Figure 4.24 provides a syntax for control types, for value holders.

```
var cData = {
            "Customer":[
                        {"cno":"1231", "cname":"Mazut"},
                        {"cno":"1232", "cname":"Motier"},
                        {"cno":"1233", "cname":"Pirdtt"}
                        ]
            };
var oModel = new sap.ui.model.json.JSONModel();
    oModel.setData(cData);
    sap.ui.getCore().setModel(oModel);

var oTemplate = new sap.ui.core.ListItem({text:"{cname}"});
```

Figure 4.24: Control types - value holders

Value holder controls (code and output)

The explanations below provide details regarding value holder controls.

AutoComplete*

(sap.ui.commons)

► gives suggestions for text completion

```
sap.ui.commons.AutoComplete({
        items:{
        path:"/Customer",
        template: oTemplate
                }
});
```

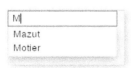

69

ComboBox*

(sap.ui.commons, sap.m)

► allows users to select an entry from a predefined list of items

```
sap.ui.commons.ComboBox({
    items:{
      path: "/Customer",
    template: oTemplate
        }
    });
```

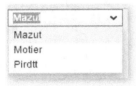

DatePicker

(sap.ui.commons, sap.m)

► gives users the ability to select a date

```
sap.ui.commons.DatePicker({
      yyyymmdd: 20151204
    });
```

70

DropdownBox*

(sap.ui.commons)

▶ consists of a down arrow

▶ allows users to select an entry from a given list

▶ users can't type in the DropdownBox

```
sap.ui.commons.DropdownBox({
    items:{
      path: "/Customer",
      template: oTemplate
          }
    });
```

PasswordField

(sap.ui.commons)

▶ displays text in a masked format

```
sap.ui.commons.PasswordField({
    design: "Monospace"
});
```

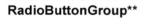

RadioButtonGroup**

(sap.ui.commons,sap.m)

▶ to group multiple radio buttons

```
sap.ui.commons.RadioButtonGroup({ columns: 1 });
.......addItem(..Item);
.......addItem(..Item);
```

CheckBox

(sap.ui.commons.sap.m)

► to select multiple options

```
sap.ui.commons.CheckBox({
     text: "Checkbox",
     checked: true,
   });
```

RangeSlider

(sap.ui.commons)

► users move the pointer to define a range

```
sap.ui.commons.RangeSlider({
        height: "100%",
        min: 0,
        max: 50,
        value: 10,
        width: "150px"
     });
```

SearchField

(sap.ui.commons,sap.m)

▶ enables a search trigger

```
sap.ui.commons.SearchField({
    enableCache: true,
    enableListSuggestion:true,
    maxSuggestionItems: 10,
    showExternalButton: false,
    showListExpander: true,
    });
```

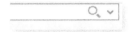

TextArea

(sap.ui.commons,sap.m)

▶ allows users to enter a large amount of text

```
sap.ui.commons.TextArea({
    editable: true,
    placeholder:"Any Comments",
    height: "50px",
    width: "150px"
    });
```

TextField

(sap.ui.commons)

► to enter text

```
sap.ui.commons.TextField({
    Value: "Text Field"
    }):
```

ValueHelpField

(sap.ui.commons)

► field with attached icon for triggering a help event

```
sap.ui.commons.ValueHelpField({
    value: "Help Field",
    valueHelpRequest: fn()…,
    });
```

DateTimeInput

(sap.m)

► gives users the ability to select a date or time

```
sap.ui.commons.DateTimeInput({
    type: "Time",
    width: "150px"
    });
```

MultiComboBox*

(sap.m)

► gives a list of pre-defined items, where multiple selections can be made

```
sap.m.MultiComboBox({
    width: "200px",
    items: {
        path: "/Customer",
        template: oTemplate
    }
});
```

*Data binding used

4.3.3   Complex control

Application header

This control is used in the header section on any page. It consists of a log-off button, welcome text and company logo/name options that are configurable according to individual requirements. The output for the application header is shown in Figure 4.25.

Example of application header

```
var oApplicationHeader = new
sap.ui.commons.ApplicationHeader("oApplicationHeader",{
    displayLogoff: true,
    displayWelcome: true,
    logoText: "Application Header",
    userName: "User1",
    logoff: function(oEvent) {
        //Some Action
    }
});
```

Figure 4.25: Example output for application header

Menu bar

A menu bar provides a user interface where MenuItems along with their Menu are arranged in a structured manner.

Example of MenuBar

```
var oMenuBar = new sap.ui.commons.MenuBar("oMenuBar",{
    design: "Header",
    enabled: true,
    width: "100%"
});
```

Menu item

A menu item is a part of the menu hierarchy; used within a menu bar of a menu or a sub-menu. The example below shows the syntax for a Menu-Item and the output is shown in Figure 4.26

Example of MenuItem

```
var oMenuItem = new sap.ui.commons.MenuItem("oMenuItem",{
    visible: true,
    text: "File",
    startsSection: false,
    enabled: true
});
oMenuBar.addItem(oMenuItem);  //
```

File

Figure 4.26: Output for MenuItem

Menu

A menu acts like a container and creates a pop-up display on the application. Menu items are mostly implemented within this. The example below shows syntax for designing a Menu and the output is shown in Figure 4.27.

Example of Menu

```
var oMenu = new sap.ui.commons.Menu("oMenu",{
    enabled: true,
    pageSize: 5
});
oMenuItem.setSubmenu(oMenu);
var oMenuItem2 = new sap.ui.commons.MenuItem("oMenuItem2",{
    enabled: true,
    startsSection: false,
    text: "New",
    visible: true
});
oMenu.addItem(oMenuItem2); //
```

Figure 4.27: Output for Menu

Menu button

A menu button is a GUI button that opens a menu when you click on it. The below example gives the syntax flow of MenuButton and Figure 4.28 shows the corresponding output.

Example of MenuButton

```
var oMenuButton = new
sap.ui.commons.MenuButton("oMenuButton",{
    icon: "sap-icon://drill-down",
    iconFirst: true,
```

```
        style: "Emph",
        styled: true,
        text: "Menu Button",
        visible: true
});
var oMenu2 = new sap.ui.commons.Menu("oMenu2",{
        pageSize: 5,
        enabled: true
});
oMenuButton.setMenu(oMenu2);
```

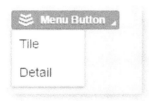

Figure 4.28: Output for menu button

Accordion

An accordion consists of multiple sections where each section can have a title and content. Sections can be dragged and compressed, or expanded, by setting properties on certain attributes. Refer to the below example for accordion syntax. The output is shown in Figure 4.29.

Example of accordion

```
var oAccordion = new sap.ui.commons.Accordion("oAccordion",{
        width: "200px"
});
var oAccordionSection = new
sap.ui.commons.AccordionSection("oAccordionSection",{
        collapsed: false,
        maxHeight: "200px",
        title: "Section 1"
});
oAccordion.addSection(oAccordionSection);
```

```
var oVerticalLayout = new
sap.ui.layout.VerticalLayout("oVerticalLayout",{
    visible: true,
    enabled: true
});
oAccordionSection.addContent(oVerticalLayout);
var oTextView = new sap.ui.commons.TextView("oTextView",{
    design: "Italic",
    enabled: true,
    text: "Inside Section 1",
    visible: true,
    wrapping: true
});
oVerticalLayout.addContent(oTextView);
var oTextArea = new sap.ui.commons.TextArea("oTextArea",{
    design: "Standard",
    editable: false,
    height: "100px",
    value: "Sections are draggable and can be collapsed"
});
oVerticalLayout.addContent(oTextArea);
var oAccordionSection1 = new
sap.ui.commons.AccordionSection("oAccordionSection1",{
    collapsed: false,
    enabled: true,
    title: "Section 2"
});
oAccordion.addSection(oAccordionSection1);
var oCheckBox = new sap.ui.commons.CheckBox("oCheckBox",{
    checked: true,
    editable: true,
    text: "Checkbox"
});
oAccordionSection1.addContent(oCheckBox);
```

Figure 4.29: Output for accordion

Carousel

A carousel is used to hold multiple controls which are displayed horizontally or vertically. Switching or navigating between controls is done via buttons or keys. A Carousel can be designed using the below example and the output appears as in Figure 4.30.

Example of carousel

```
var oCarousel = new sap.ui.commons.Carousel("oCarousel",{
    width: "300px",
    orientation: "horizontal",
    height: "200px",
    handleSize: 22,
    firstVisibleIndex: 0,
    defaultItemWidth: 150,
    defaultItemHeight: 150,
    animationDuration: 500
});
var oTable = new sap.m.Table("oTable",{
    width: "300px",
    visible: true,
    showNoData: true,
    rememberSelections: true,
    modeAnimationOn: true,
    inset: false,
```

```
        includeItemInSelection: false,
        headerText: "Student Table",
        headerDesign: "Standard",
        growingThreshold: 20,
        growingScrollToLoad: false,
        growing: false,
        fixedLayout: true
});
oCarousel.addContent(oTable); // Continue adding columns..
```

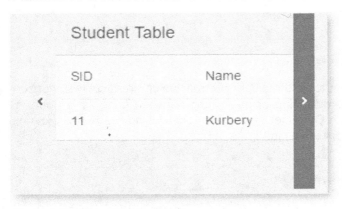

Figure 4.30: Output for Carousel

Segmented button

A segmented button displays a group of buttons, where only one can be
selected at a time. See the example below for segmented button syntax
and Figure 4.31 for the corresponding output.

Example of segmented button

```
var oSegmentedButton = new
sap.ui.commons.SegmentedButton("oSegmentedButton",{
    visible: true,
    enabled: true
});
var oButton = new sap.ui.commons.Button("oButton",{
```

```
    icon: "sap-icon://activate",
    style: "Accept",
    styled: true,
    width: "50px"
});
oSegmentedButton.addButton(oButton);
var oButton1 = new sap.ui.commons.Button("oButton1",{
    enabled: true,
    icon: "sap-icon://save",
    style: "Default",
    styled: true,
    visible: true,
    width: "50px"
});
oSegmentedButton.addButton(oButton1);
```

Figure 4.31: Output for segmented button

Progress indicator

A progress indicator shows the progress of any process in a GUI bar format. The values for the bar can be hidden or set to any numerical value. Below is the syntax for a progress indicator design and Figure 4.32 shows the corresponding output.

Example of progress indicator

```
var oProgressIndicator = new
sap.ui.commons.ProgressIndicator("oProgressIndicator",{
    barColor: "POSITIVE",
    displayValue: "46%",
    percentValue: 46,
    showValue: true,
    visible: true,
    width: "200px"
});
```

Figure 4.32: Output for progress indicator

Paginator

A paginator provides options for switching between a number of pages within an application. Refer to the below example for paginator syntax and its output in Figure 4.33.

Example of paginator

```
var oPaginator = new sap.ui.commons.Paginator("oPaginator",{
    currentPage: 1,
    numberOfPages: 3
});
```

Figure 4.33: Output for paginator

4.3.4   SAP UX3/ Shell controls

Shell and Shell Item

A shell is an application frame with navigation functionality. On the left side of a shell frame a search and feeder option is available which can also be hidden. Similarly, additional controls like a pane can be added to the other side of the frame; header items such as heading and menu options or controls can be arranged in any layout inside a shell area.

See the below example for shell controls. The corresponding output is shown in Figure 4.34.

Example of shell controls

```
var oShell = new sap.ui.ux3.Shell("oShell",{
    appTitle: "SAP UX3 Shell",
    applyContentPadding: true,
    paneWidth: 250,
    showFeederTool: true,
    showLogoutButton: true,
    showPane: true,
    showSearchTool: true,
    showTools: true
});
oShell.placeAt("body");
var oLabel = new sap.ui.commons.Label("oLabel",{
    design: "Bold",
    required: false,
    text: "Header Item",
    visible: true,
    wrapping: false
});
oShell.addHeaderItem(oLabel);
```

Figure 4.34: Output for shell and shell item

Collection inspector/ Collection item

A collection inspector consists of a header bar where multiple items can be arranged. On selecting an appropriate item, a sidebar with sub-items appears. This side-bar can be closed or opened with a click. Refer to the below example for collection inspector and collection items; the corresponding output is shown in Figure 4.35.

Example of collection inspector and items

```
var oCollectionInspector = new
sap.ui.ux3.CollectionInspector("oCollectionInspector",{
    fitParent: true,
    sidebarVisible: true,
    visible: true
});
oCollectionInspector.placeAt("body");
var oCollection = new sap.ui.ux3.Collection("oCollection",{
    editable: false,
    multiSelection: false,
    title: "Quick Links"
});
oCollectionInspector.addCollection(oCollection);
var oCollectionItem = new
sap.ui.core.Item("oCollectionItem",{
    enabled: true,
    text: "Mail"
});
oCollection.addItem(oCollectionItem);
var oCollectionItem1 = new
sap.ui.core.Item("oCollectionItem1",{
    enabled: true,
    text: "Site"
});
oCollection.addItem(oCollectionItem1);....
```

Figure 4.35: Output for collection inspector/ collection item

Navigation bar / Navigation items

A navigation bar is presented on a horizontal line with navigation items over it, as options. A selected item is highlighted and surrounded by a dashed outline. Within each navigation item a new body content is created and can be filled with various controls and layouts. Refer to the below example for navigation bar and items syntax. The output can be seen in Figure 4.36.

Example of navigation bar and items

```
var oNavigationBar = new
sap.ui.ux3.NavigationBar("oNavigationBar",{
    toplevelVariant: true
});
oNavigationBar.placeAt("body");
var oNavigationItem = new
sap.ui.ux3.NavigationItem("oNavigationItem",{
    enabled: true,
```

```
        text: "Home"
});
oNavigationBar.addItem(oNavigationItem);
var oNavigationItem1 = new
sap.ui.ux3.NavigationItem("oNavigationItem1",{
        enabled: true,
        text: "Products"
});
oNavigationBar.addItem(oNavigationItem1);
```

Figure 4.36: Output for Navigation Bar / Navigation Items

Notification bar

A notification bar appears on the bottom of a screen to display messages for a current transaction. Its style properties (i.e. color, position, height and width) can be changed using CSS classes. To display a particular type of message Notifier control is used. The latest messages appear at the top and have color notations for the various types of messages (i.e. red for error, yellow for warning, etc.). See the below example for notification bar syntax and its output in Figure 4.37.

Example of notification bar

```
var oNotificationBar = new
sap.ui.ux3.NotificationBar("oNotificationBar",{
        resizeEnabled: true,
        visibleStatus: "Default"
});
oNotificationBar.placeAt("body");
var oNotifier = new sap.ui.ux3.Notifier("oNotifier",{
        title: "Notifications"
});
```

```
oNotificationBar.addNotifier(oNotifier);
oNotificationBar.setMessageNotifier(oNotifier);
var oNotificationMessage = new
sap.ui.core.Message("oNotificationMessage",{
    level: "Success",
    readOnly: false,
    text: "Password Changed Successfully"
});
oNotifier.addMessage(oNotificationMessage);
```

Figure 4.37: Output for notification bar

Overlay container

An overlay container is a pop-up display which appears over the application content. Events such as "open" and "close" can be attached over this container.

The below example shows the container syntax and the output can be seen in Figure 4.38.

Example of overlay container

```
var oButton = new sap.ui.commons.Button("oButton",{
    enabled: true,
    styled: true,
    text: "Button",
    visible: true,
    press: function(oEvent) {
        // oThingInspector.open();
        oOverlayContainer.open();
    }
```

```
});
oButton.placeAt("body");
var oOverlayContainer = new
sap.ui.ux3.OverlayContainer("oOverlayContainer",{
    closeButtonVisible: true,
    openButtonVisible: true,
    visible: true,
    close: function(oEvent) {
        alert('close');
    }
});
var oLabel3 = new sap.ui.commons.Label("oLabel3",{
    design: "Bold",
    text: "Label Inside Container"
});
oOverlayContainer.addContent(oLabel3);
```

Label Inside Container

Figure 4.38: Output for overlay container

4.3.5 Custom Controls

As we have seen, there are numerous controls within the OpenUI5 library. However, when we are unable to find a particular control required for a business scenario, controls can be modified by adding the *.extend* property at the end of the constructor function; for example, for a Button control sap.ui.commons.Button.extend or, for an entire core class, sap.ui.core.Control.extend.

Basically, the *.extend* method extends the functionality of a control or creates an entirely new control. For a custom control, its constructor consists of metadata, event handlers, public/private methods and the renderer method. Figure 4.39 shows how custom controls can be created.

```
sap.ui.core.Control.extend("ControlName", {
            metadata : {
                properties: {},
                events: {},
                aggregations: {}
            },
            publicMethod: function() {},
            privateMethod: function() {},
            init: function() {},
            renderer: function() {}
});
```

Figure 4.39: Example of custom control

5 SAP Fiori

SAP Fiori is a new user experience for SAP applications, software and products. Fiori applications are created with five design principles in mind:

- ▶ Role-based—different applications or separate privileges can be given to a user or group of similar users.
- ▶ Responsiveness—arranges application content dynamically based on the screen size or device type.
- ▶ Simple—this is easy to understand and operate, because fewer clicks and fewer screens with beautiful designs are available.
- ▶ Seamless experience—this can run on any applicable language, regardless of platform and deployment scenario.
- ▶ Delightful—Fiori can be deployed on SAP ECC 6.0 ERP central component and higher-version system, thus making it easier to use.

5.1 Fiori applications

An *SAP Fiori* application consists of a UI component and an integration component. The UI component deals with all OpenUI5 development and integration components with an SAP NetWeaver Gateway service. SAP Fiori applications are classified into three categories.

5.1.1 Transactional applications

Transactional applications are used to perform transaction tasks such as create, change and display. These applications allow users to run widely-used SAP transactions on mobile devices and various platforms.

The first set of Fiori applications released were transactional apps. See Figure 5.1 for transactional application layout.

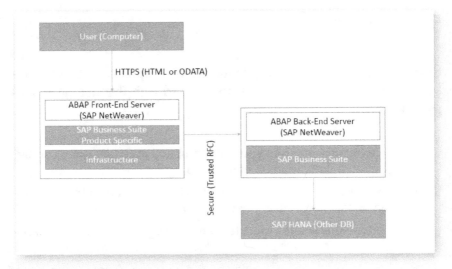

Figure 5.1: Transactional application layout

With regard to architecture, transactional applications run efficiently on a HANA database. They also support other databases, only minimally affecting performance. The connection between an ABAP front-end server and an ABAP back-end server is via a trusted remote function call (RFC) connection, where the front-end consists of UI-components for products such as CRM, SCM and an infrastructure component in which lies within the OpenUI5 library, Fiori launchpad and SAP NetWeaver Gateway. The ABAP backend server is the place where business logic is located and is connected through RFC to a respective database.

Examples of transactional applications are leave requests, travel requests, and purchase orders.

5.1.2   Fact sheets

Fact sheets are applications that display contextual information and all details about ongoing and completed business operations. Fact sheets applications can only run on a HANA database and require an ABAP stack with it. Navigation between different facts sheets or transactional applications can be done using these facts sheets applications. Figure 5.2 shows a fact sheets layout.

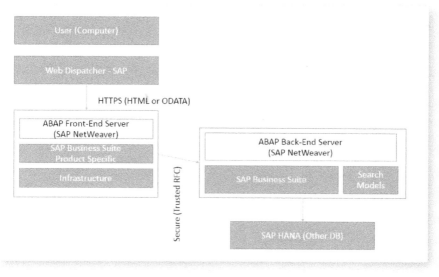

Figure 5.2 : Fact sheets layout

With regard to architecture, the ABAP front-end and back-end are con-nected through a trusted RFC connection. An additional layer called a web dispatcher is used in fact sheets which sends HTTPS requests to servers. In this architecture, the ABAP back-end server consists of search models which provide search results according to user require-ments. An example of fact sheets would be a display detailing customers and their related vendors, contracts, etc.

5.1.3 Analytical applications

Analytical applications are role-based applications which collect and display key information derived from real-time business operations on the client side. Web dispatcher is the first layer of contact, holding an HTTP/HTTPS request, and decides whether to send the request to the ABAP front-end server or to the HANA XS engine. Figure 5.3 gives a layout overview for analytical applications.

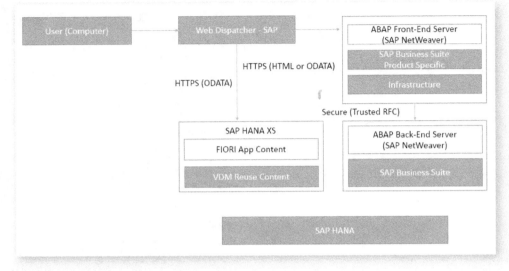

Figure 5.3 : Analytical application layout

The architecture for analytical applications contains 5 components: web dispatcher, ABAP front-end server, ABAP back-end server, HANA XS engine and HANA database.

5.2 Fiori launchpad and theme designer

5.2.1 SAP Fiori launchpad

SAP Fiori launchpad is the starting point for Fiori applications. Launchpad consists of single or multiple tiles of different shapes (e.g. square or rectangle) and navigates to its assigned application on clicking; it is supported on multiple devices. Different tiles appear for different users depending on their role.

The key principles of Fiori launchpad are:

▶ Simple—attractive appearance, easy and readable

▶ Role-based—options are available to assigned users

- ▶ Responsive—customizable, updates dynamically and adjusts according to any device
- ▶ Multi-platform—it is applied on ABAP, SAP HANA, SAP HANA Cloud and SAP portal

Figure 5.4 gives you a view of the layout of the launchpad.

The transaction code for customizing the launchpad in SAP is LPD_CUST.

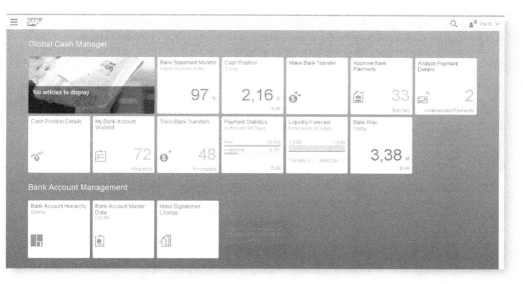

Figure 5.4: Sample layout for launchpad

Tiles are customizable and can be embellished by combining other controls over them. Contents on a tile change dynamically depending on the binding mode. To create a launchpad for a set of applications, the URL should be created in the formats shown below.

Launchpad:

https://<host>.<domain>:<port>/sap/bc/ui5_ui5/ui2/ushell/shells/abap/ Fiorilaunchpad.html?sap-client=<client>&sap-language=EN.

Launchpad designer:

https://<host>.<domain>:<port>/sap/bc/ui5_ui5/sap/arsrvc_upb_admn/ main.html?sap-client=<Client>?scope=CUST.

Fiori launchpad consists of 3 components:

▶ *Tile*—a box or set of boxes, which we see on the screen. On clicking a specific tile, its corresponding application is launched.

▶ *Catalog*—consists of a list of applications in launchpad, displayed in a list format on the right-hand panel on the screen. Applications are searchable and are sorted according to usage. The layout can be seen in Figure 5.5.

Figure 5.5 : Catalog layout

▶ *Group*—consists of a set or a group of related or role-based applications for users.

A few more features can also be used in launchpad such as dynamic tiles for updating information at set time intervals, or adding RSS feeds to show updated information or any changes in application.

Fiori provides a tool called Theme Designer (runs on browser) which allows users to customize or create new themes, thereby changing the visual appearance of an application according to requirements.

The key features of Theme Designer are:

▶ theme parameters—can be changed within the tool and all the changes take place instantaneously

▶ built-in preview option— for individual pages and for the whole application

Theme designer can be accessed either by entering the SAP transaction code /UI5/THEME_DESIGNER or by entering the URL *http(s)://<server>:<port>/sap/bc/theming/theme-designer?sap-client= <client>* in the browser. Figure 5.6 shows the procedure to select themes in theme designer.

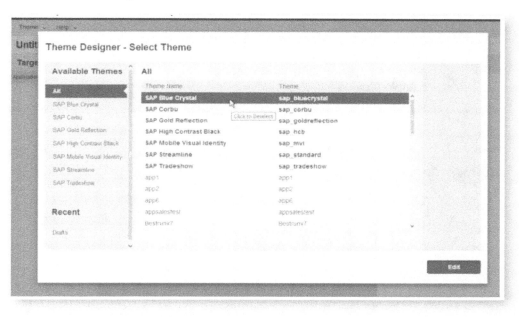

Figure 5.6: Theme designer—selection of themes

▶ On the screen, a list of templates provided by SAP are displayed. Select a theme and click on 'Edit'.

▶ Provide your application URL and Name. Click on 'Add' to proceed. Refer to Figure 5.7 to add target content.

Add Target Content

Application

Link to Application: |

Name of Application:

Add

Test Suites

UR Control Previews

NWBC Applications Previews

Figure 5.7: Adding target content

▶ Your application will appear inside the Theme Designer. On the right side, under 'Quick' tab, we can change colors, font sizes and images (e.g. company logo). Expert and CSS tabs give us advanced options for discrete changes. Figure 5.8 shows a sample preview.

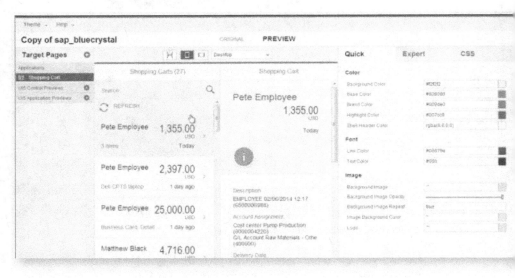

Figure 5.8: Sample preview

5.3 SAP NetWeaver Gateway

SAP NetWeaver Gateway is a simple technology that allows us to connect various devices, platforms and environments to SAP software. From a client application developer's perspective, the SAP Gateway interface doesn't require any complex technical understanding. Gateway is considered an ABAP add-on within the SAP business suite system, where its primary role is to make business data available on request. On the whole, it acts like a middleman between the business suite and target clients (browser, mobile applications), providing an API that uses an OData protocol. See Figure 5.9 for SAP NetWeaver Gateway architecture.

Any add-on into the SAP system is done via a SAINT transaction.

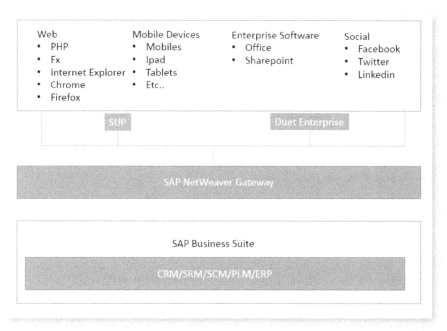

Figure 5.9: SAP NetWeaver Gateway

Deployment of SAP Gateway can be done in two ways: embedded deployment and central-hub deployment. In embedded deployment, SAP Gateway, together with optional backend components and SAP Business Suite, are installed on the same system; keep in mind that the business suite should meet certain requirements to support Gateway. Using this deployment method, we can reduce runtime complexity and no separate central hub system is required. For this deployment, the core Gateway components installed on the Business Suite backend are IW_FND and GW_CORE. The backend of the gateway can be seen in Figure 5.10. Some of the advantages of embedded deployment are:

▶ low maintenance costs—only one system is used

▶ direct access to business and metadata

▶ less runtime—one RFC call is reduced

Figure 5.10: SAP NetWeaver Gateway backend

With standalone development, deployment configuration becomes a little more complex because SAP Gateway, along with optional backend components, are installed in a standalone system (separate) which can be used on multiple Business Suites. Depending on the NetWeaver version, components can be installed either on the Business Suite or a standalone system; for example, for NW version 7.02 to 7.31, component IW_BEP is used. Some of the advantages of NetWeaver Gateway are:

▶ multiple systems supported for routing

▶ one-time deployment

▶ dedicated gateway content is available, which speeds up individual systems

▶ better security

Figure 5.11 illustrates the SAP NetWeaver Gateway backend standalone development.

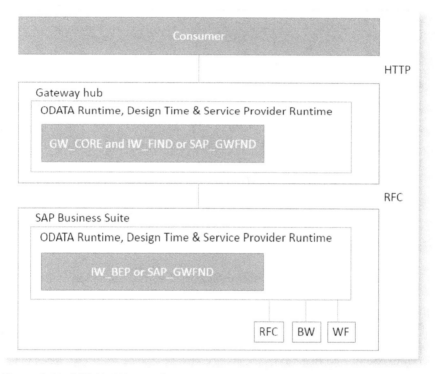

Figure 5.11: SAP NetWeaver Gateway backend standalone development

The core component IW_FND provides the main functionalities of Gateway such metadata storage, monitoring services and runtime components. The GW_CORE component holds OData libraries. The SAP_GWFND component is used for NW version 7.40 or higher; it provides the combined functionality of IW_FND, GW_CORE and IW_BEP. The IW_BEP component is only used on a Gateway deployed on the central hub for enabling OData services. Figure 5.12 shows how to check the component version.

To check which deployment method is installed in your system:

▶ Go to the home screen and click on *System*.

▶ Select the *Status* option.

▶ Click on a button with a search icon on it, as shown in the image below.

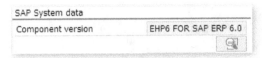

Figure 5.12: SAP system data component version

▶ A list of the components installed on the back-end system appears in a new window.

▶ Look for components corresponding to their NW version.

5.4 OData, REST and RFC Connection

5.4.1 OData

OData protocol was developed by Microsoft as an extension to the Atom Publishing and Atom Syndication protocols, but is now administered by the Oasis Organization. OData protocol is built over HTTP and REST (Representational State Transfer) protocols which are useful for creating and consuming RESTful API's through the use of CRUD (create, read, update, delete) operations.

OData works based on a lifecycle for its service. A lifecycle involves:

▶ activation of services

▶ maintenance of services

▶ maintenance of services and models

▶ metadata cache

To utilize OData services, you use SAP NetWeaver Gateway Service Builder, which is a design environment provided by SAP. The transaction code for Service Builder is SEGW and it consists of a set of tools that support development throughout the lifecycle of a service. For installation of this tool in a system lower than NetWeaver 7.40, IW_BEP is required, and for 7.40 or higher, you need SAP_GWFND.

5.4.2   REST

REST stands for Representational State Transfer. REST is a preferred design model because of its simpler style and support of various HTTP protocols and standard methods such as GET, POST, PUT and DELETE. When web services use REST architecture they are called RESTful API'S. These APIs consume less bandwidth on networks and are stateless (i.e. they don't store any records of interactions in a network).

REST architecture HTTP methods and OData CRUD operations can be mapped as follows:

- ▶ To create a new resource on the server, use POST.
- ▶ To retrieve a resource from the server, use GET.
- ▶ To change or update any resource, use PUT.
- ▶ To remove any resource, use DELETE.

The HTTP mapping method with CRUD can be seen in Table 5.1.

HTTP Method	CRUD Method
POST	Create
GET	Read
PUT	Update
DELETE	Delete

Table 5.1: Mapping HTTP method with CRUD method

We take the existing OData service available online which can be accessed through the following example URL:

http://services.OData.org/OData/OData.svc/

```
▼<service xmlns="http://www.w3.org/2007/app" xmlns:atom="http://www.w3.org/2005/Atom"
  xml:base="http://services.odata.org/OData/OData.svc/">
  ▼<workspace>
    <atom:title>Default</atom:title>
    ▶<collection href="Products">...</collection>
    ▶<collection href="ProductDetails">...</collection>
    ▶<collection href="Categories">...</collection>
    ▶<collection href="Suppliers">...</collection>
    ▶<collection href="Persons">...</collection>
    ▶<collection href="PersonDetails">...</collection>
    ▶<collection href="Advertisements">...</collection>
  </workspace>
</service>
```

Figure 5.13: OData service example

To help understand the content, Figure 5.13 shows OData sample data in XML format—it consists of 7 different entity sets (between the <collection> tag). To retrieve the desired data from the above source, OData follows the URL scheme, as shown in Figure 5.14.

Figure 5.14: URL format for working on OData

The service root URI is the hosting service for OData service. This is followed by the **resource path**, where we mention what resources we are considering from the service. Finally, come the **query options**, where we tell the service to return a particular entity or to sort a set of data.

If you want to comprehend any number of the entity sets, add slash "/" followed by the entity set name to the suffix of the URL. To get metadata (full structure of the data) for the above service, add *$metadata* to the suffix of the URL:

(*http://services.OData.org/OData/OData.svc/$metadata*)—this yields a metadata model for the OData above.

A metadata model starts with EDMX (Entity Data Model Specification) which describes a way to interpret a metadata operation. Here we take a small portion of the entity set 'ProductDetail' metadata and describe its following representations:

```
▼<EntityType Name="ProductDetail">
  ▼<Key>
     <PropertyRef Name="ProductID"/>
  </Key>
  <Property Name="ProductID" Type="Edm.Int32" Nullable="false"/>
  <Property Name="Details" Type="Edm.String"/>
  <NavigationProperty Name="Product"
  Relationship="ODataDemo.Product_ProductDetail_ProductDetail_Product"
  ToRole="Product_ProductDetail" FromRole="ProductDetail_Product"/>
</EntityType>
```

Figure 5.15: Product detail entity set

Below are the points defining the different tags in Figure 5.15:

▶ <Key> tag for primary (unique) key—here, *ProductID* is the primary key.

▶ <Property> tag for entity set contents, data-types and properties—as we can see, *ProductID* has data type *Int32* and *Details* data type is *String*.

▶ <NavigationProperty> shows the relationship of this entity set with other entity sets, such as how Product and ProductDetails are related.

Figure 5.16 shows the output of the query written in Figure 5.15.

By default, data is returned in XML format. To view it in JSON format, add the suffix *$format=json* to the URL. So, to read the ProductDetails data in JSON format, the URL is framed as:

http://services.OData.org/OData/OData.svc/ProductDetails?$format=json

```
{"odata.metadata":"http://services.odata.org/OData/OData.svc
/$metadata#ProductDetails","value":
[{"ProductID":1,"Details":"Details of product 1"},
{"ProductID":3,"Details":"Details of product 3"},
{"ProductID":4,"Details":"Details of product 4"},
{"ProductID":8,"Details":"Details of product 8"}]}
```

Figure 5.16: Result of the query

The most commonly used queries on OData are listed below:

- ▶ $select—used for selecting a specific field from all fields present in an entity set
http://serv.............$format=json&$select=ID,Description

- ▶ $orderby—used for sorting entity data in either ascending or descending order
http://service.........................$orderby=Name desc

- ▶ $expand—used for retrieving multiple sets of data in a single client request
http://services.OData.org/OData/OData.svc/Products?$expand= Categories&$format=json

5.4.3 Remote function call (RFC)

RFC is a type of function module used for remote communication between servers; the servers can be SAP or non-SAP. To set up communication between two different SAP systems, an RFC destination is required. The transaction code for creating an RFC connection is SM59.

The basic procedure to setup Gateway is as follows:

- ▶ Go to transaction SM59.
- ▶ Click on create icon.
- ▶ Provide an RFC destination name, connection type and description (optional). Refer to Figure 5.17.
- ▶ Under the Technical Settings tab, enter Gateway Host (target host) and system number in the field.
- ▶ Under the Login & Security tab enter the logon credentials with an appropriate password and set Trust Relationship to *Yes*.
- ▶ To test the connection, click on the Connection Test button on the application bar.
- ▶ Now navigate to transaction SMT1 to build a trust relationship for various systems. Click on the Create icon to open the trusting Wizard.

▶ Enter the RFC destination name created above in the Enter destination option and click Continue.

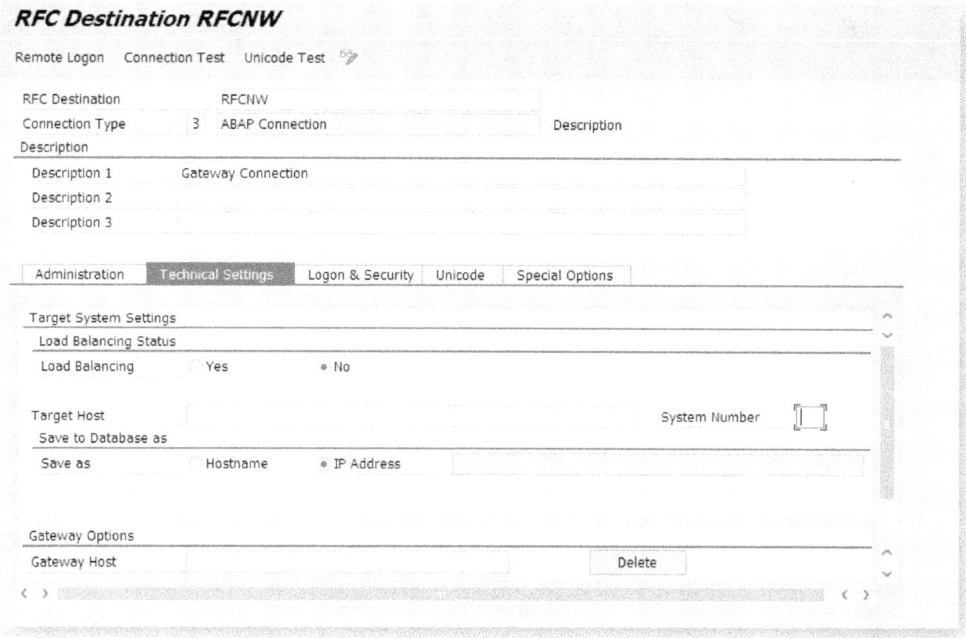

RFC Destination RFCNW

Remote Logon   Connection Test   Unicode Test

RFC Destination		RFCNW		
Connection Type	3	ABAP Connection		Description
Description				
Description 1		Gateway Connection		
Description 2				
Description 3				

Administration	Technical Settings	Logon & Security	Unicode	Special Options

Target System Settings
  Load Balancing Status

  Load Balancing   Yes   ● No

Target Host   System Number   [   ]
  Save to Database as

  Save as   Hostname   ● IP Address   [   ]

Gateway Options

  Gateway Host   [   ]   [Delete]

Figure 5.17: RFC connection setup

6 Application Development

6.1 Mobile application

Navigation within a mobile application is achieved by using two commonly used controls—sap.m.App and sap.m.NavContainer. These controls come under the layout category because they are responsible for framing an application according to screen-size and pixel-count.

Control sap.m.NavContainer handles hierarchical navigation between pages and shares navigation properties with sap.m.App.

We often use sap.m.App as a root (parent) control and place multiple pages within it. This makes it possible to manage navigation between pages. By default, whatever page is added first within sap.m.App, it becomes the first page of an application and remaining pages appear according to the assigned navigation events. Events related to navigation are triggered by either App/NavContainer or by a before/after display of pages. Figure 6.1 shows an example of a mobile application navigation and its output can be seen in Figure 6.2 and Figure 6.3.

```
var App = new sap.m.App("App",{
    defaultTransitionName: "slide",
    height: "100%",
    width: "100%"
});
App.placeAt("content");
var mainPage = new sap.m.Page("mainPage",{
    backgroundDesign: "Standard",
    title: "PAGE 1"
});
App.addPage(mainPage);
var oButton4 = new sap.m.Button("oButton4",{
    text: "Navigate",
    press: function(oEvent) {
        App.to(secondPage, "flip");
    }
});
mainPage.addContent(oButton4);
var secondPage = new sap.m.Page("secondPage",{
    navButtonType: "Back",
    showHeader: true,
    showNavButton: true,
    title: "PAGE 2",
    navButtonPress: function(oEvent) {
        App.back();
    }
});
App.addPage(secondPage);
```

Figure 6.1: Mobile application navigation example

Figure 6.2: Mobile application navigation example output—page 1

Figure 6.3: Mobile application navigation example output—page 2

sap.m.SplitApp is another UI5 control which can be used as a root element. SplitApp consists of 2 NavContainers called master view and detail view. The master page (as shown in Figure 6.4) appears on the left side and has a fixed size, whereas the detail page is on the right side and has a dynamic size. The size for these pages changes according to device size. In almost every mobile device, the detail page is hidden and is present under a master page; for tablet/desktop devices both the pages appear simultaneously. The output for the SplitApp example can be seen in Figure 6.5 and a rotated view is shown in Figure 6.6.

Navigation in sap.m.SplitApp is done using the splitApp.toMaster() and splitApp.backDetail() methods.

```
var oPageM = new sap.m.Page("oPageM",{
            backgroundDesign: "Solid",
            title: "MASTER PAGE"
            });
var oButton4 = new sap.m.Button("oButton4",{
             text: "Navigate",
             press: function(oEvent) {
                 oSplitApp.toDetail(oPageD);
                 }
             });
        oPageM.addContent(oButton4);
var oPageD = new sap.m.Page("oPageD",{
             backgroundDesign: "Transparent",
             navButtonType: "Back",
             showNavButton: true,
             title: "DETAIL PAGE",
             navButtonPress: function(oEvent) {
                 // oSplitApp.toMaster(oPageM)
                 oSplitApp.backMaster();
                 }
             });
var oSplitApp = new sap.m.SplitApp("oSplitApp",{
              detailPages: [oPageD],
              masterPages: [oPageM],
              defaultTransitionNameDetail: "slide",
              defaultTransitionNameMaster: "slide",
              });
if (sap.ui.Device.system.phone) {
    oSplitApp.to(oPageM, "show");
    }
oSplitApp.placeAt("content");
```

Figure 6.4: Navigation via SplitApp

Figure 6.5: Navigation through SplitApp output

Figure 6.6: Navigation through SplitApp—output rotated

The UI5 framework provides a device and feature detection API in namespace sap.ui.Device; this is primarily used for assigning touching, swiping, resizing or orientation change events on different devices. The following is a list of some of the classes within this namespace:

▶ browser—information about the current browser (Chrome, Mozilla)

▶ orientation— changing orientation view for the device (landscape or portrait)

▶ OS—information about the current OS (Android, iOS)

▶ support—contains features of the browser or device (touch, retina)

▶ system— categorization of the current device (tablet, phone, desktop)

Refer to Figure 6.7 for an example of sap.ui.Device.

```
if(sap.ui.Device.system.tablet || sap.ui.Device.system.desktop){
    oPageD.setShowNavButton(false);
}
```

Figure 6.7: Code to hide the back button if the device is a desktop or a tablet

In our above example, we can add this piece of code to hide the back button on the detail page if the device is a desktop or a tablet.

Additional types of events which can be applied before and after navigation to a page are:

▶ beforeShow—before display of the page

▶ beforeFirstShow— before display of the page, one time only

▶ beforeHide—before leaving the page

▶ afterShow—triggers after the beforeShow event (if mentioned) or when the page appears

▶ afterHide—triggers after the beforeHide event (if mentioned) or after leaving the page

```
var oNavContainer = new sap.m.NavContainer("oNavContainer",{
                        width: "100%",
                        height: "100%",
                        defaultTransitionName: "slide",

                        navigate: function(oEvent) {
                                    alert('NAVIGATE');
                            }
                        afterNavigate: function(oEvent) {
                                    alert('After NAVIGATE')
                            },

                    });
oPage.addContent(oNavContainer);
var page1 = new sap.m.Page("page1",{
                    showHeader: true,
                    title: "PAGE 1"
            });
oNavContainer.addPage(page1);
var oButton = new sap.m.Button("oButton",{
    text: "Press",
    press: function(oEvent) {
        oNavContainer.to(page2);
        }
});
```

Figure 6.8: Navigate and afterNavigate events inside a sap.m.NavContainer

In Figure 6.8, we placed navigate and afterNavigate events inside an sap.m.NavContainer.

In Chapter 5, we saw different types of layouts and controls. In addition to these, we often use tables and lists in application development to display data in a structured format. OpenUI5 provides us with both a table and a list control in sap.m library. Both controls share common properties such as grouping, selection-modes, navigation types and detection of swipe events.

A "table" consists of *n* number of horizontal rows and vertical columns. Columns are created using sap.m.Column and rows are bound to it with sap.m.ColumnListItem. For a list, it acts like a container holding different types of list items. Figure 6.9 shows an example of how to create a table and a list using sap.m controls.

Refer to Figure 6.10 for syntax to create a model for holding JSON data.

An example of a simple table is shown in Figure 6.11 and its output is in Figure 6.12.

```
"[{"KUNNR":"0000000001","NAME1":"Birmingham-
Jeffereson County","ORT01":"Birmingham"},
{"KUNNR":"0000000002","NAME1":"Knuston
Construction Services","ORT01":"Rochester"},
{"KUNNR":"0000000003","NAME1":"Magnetic
Ticket and Label","ORT01":"Dallas"}]"
```

Figure 6.9: Example—create a table and list using sap.m controls.

```
var modelData = new sap.ui.model.json.JSONModel();
modelData.loadData(//JSON file Here);
oPage1.setModel(modelData);
```

Figure 6.10: Creating a model for holding JSON data

```
var custTable = new sap.m.Table("custTable",{
        headerText: "Customer Table",
        headerDesign: "Standard",
        growing: true,
        fixedLayout: true,
        backgroundDesign: "Solid"
    });
    oPage1.addContent(custTable);

var colCust = new sap.m.Column("colCust",{
        header: new sap.m.Label({
            text: "Customer"
        })
    });
    custTable.addColumn(colCust);
    //.... Same for Name and City
    custTable.addColumn(colCity);
var colListItem1 = new sap.m.ColumnListItem("colListItem1",{
        selected: false,
        unread: false,
        type: "Active",
    });
    custTable.bindAggregation("items", "/", colListItem1);
var textCust = new sap.m.Text("textCust",{
        text: "{KUNNR}",
        wrapping: true
    });
    colListItem1.addCell(textCust);
    //....Same for Name and City
    //....
```

Figure 6.11: Code for creating a simple table with sap.m.Table

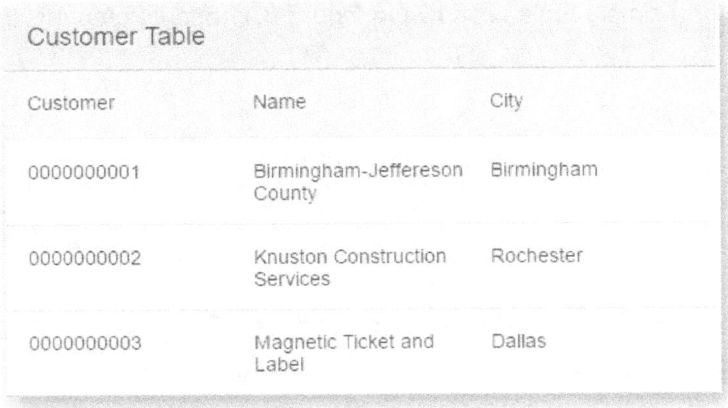

Customer Table

Customer	Name	City
0000000001	Birmingham-Jeffereson County	Birmingham
0000000002	Knuston Construction Services	Rochester
0000000003	Magnetic Ticket and Label	Dallas

Figure 6.12: Output—a table created with sap.m.Table

Additional properties can be applied to sap.m.Table to meet its require-ments—set the mode property of the table to either Multiselect, Delete or SingleSelectLeft. These properties are shown in Figure 6.13.

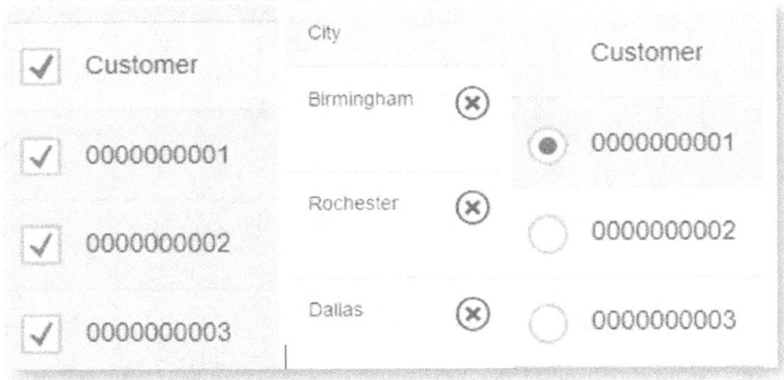

Figure 6.13: Example—table with Multiselect, Delete and SingleSelect

We sometimes have a huge amount of data resulting in many rows and columns, and it becomes challenging to display all the content on a small device (e.g. phone). For this type of situation, sap.m.Column comes with additional properties such as;

► minScreenWidth—By default a column is always visible. Using this property hides or displays a column based on screen size.

▶ demandPopin/ popinDisplay—This property displays hidden columns as pop-ins, depending on screen sizes. Using this property, we have better options to display pop-ins.

CSS functionality such as highlighting rows and columns, or specifying
width for a column, can be achieved by using the styleClass property.

```
var custList = new sap.m.List("custList",{
        growing: true,
        headerText: "Customer List"
    });
    oPage1.addContent(custList);
//Need to Create Model ...
var custListItem = new sap.m.ObjectListItem("custListItem",{
        intro: "{ORT01}",
        number: "{KUNNR}",
        numberUnit: "Customer No.",
        title: "{NAME1}",
        type: "Active"
    });
    custList.bindAggregation("items", "/", custListItem);
```

Figure 6.14: Creating a simple list with sap.n.List

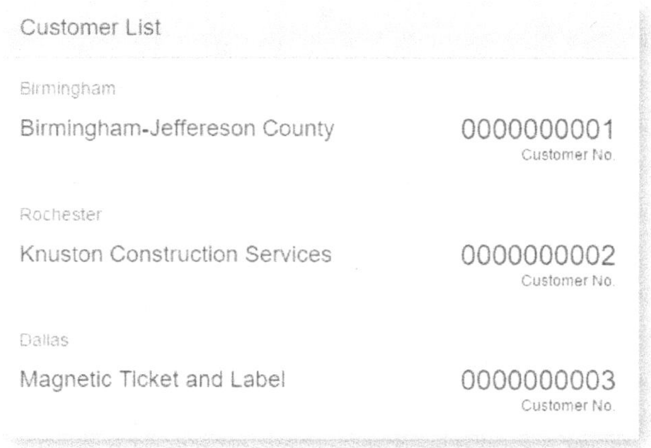

Customer List

Birmingham

Birmingham-Jeffereson County   0000000001
                                       Customer No.

Rochester

Knuston Construction Services   0000000002
                                       Customer No.

Dallas

Magnetic Ticket and Label   0000000003
                                       Customer No.

Figure 6.15: Output - simple list using sap.m.List

For sap.m.List we used sap.m.ObjectListItem to display number, name
and city as one item. Like tables, sap.m.List also supports different mode
types; i.e. MultiSelect, Delete, etc. Furthermore, additional content can

be added into a list item by using an appropriate control. To display all items in a list, set the property "growing: true". Other properties which can be applied over the growing property are growingScrollToLoad, growingThreshold and growingTriggerText. Refer to Figure 6.14 for sap.n.List and Figure 6.15 for sap.m.List.

Before setting the growing property to true for a list or table, ensure that your respective parent control (sap.m.Page) has its enableScrolling property set to true. There are four controls in OpenUI5 which support the scrolling property—Page, Scrollcontainer, Dialog and Popover.

To trigger other native mobile phone applications, we use sap.m.URLHelper to trigger native applications like phone-calls, messaging, browser or email. The URLHelper API methods can be seen in Figure 6.16.

Figure 6.16: URLHelper API methods

7 Working Examples

This section provides some working examples which will give you a better idea of how applications are created using UI5.

7.1 To display records using a list control and provide interaction

First, create an App and place a page in it which will hold the list and allow us to provide interaction. Then, create a list and define its properties, as shown in Figure 7.1.

```
var oList = new sap.m.List({
headerText:"Sales Order List",
headerDesign: "Plain",
backgroundDesign: "Transparent",
keyboardMode: "Navigation",
});
```

Figure 7.1: Create a list

Next, bind the data that should be displayed in the list. To do this, use ObjectListItem from sap.m library, as shown in Figure 7.2.

```
oList.bindItems({
path : "/sales",
template : new sap.m.ObjectListItem({
    intro: "{createdOn}",
    title: "{sNumber}",
    number: "{createdBy}",
    type: sap.m.ListType.Active,
    press:function(active){
        var binding = active.getSource().getBindingContext();
        page2.setBindingContext(binding);
        oApp.to("page2");
        }
    })
});
```

Figure 7.2: Binding items to list

Sap.m.ListType allows you to define the behavior of a list item which is set to active. To make a list item clickable, see again the example in Figure 7.2. Clicking on the list item navigates to the next page where details of the list item show up; the binding is captured and set to the next page, also shown in Figure 7.2.

Now, add a control to display the details of the list item for which a SimpleForm can be used, as shown in Figure 7.3.

```
var simpleForm = new sap.ui.layout.form.SimpleForm({
    title: "Sales order Details",
    content: [
        new sap.m.Label({text: "Sales Order Number"}),
        new sap.ui.commons.TextField({value: "{sNumber}",
                            width:"200px",
                            editable: false}),

        new sap.m.Label({text: "Created By"}),
        new sap.ui.commons.TextField({value: "{createdBy}",
                            width:"200px",
                            editable: false}),

        new sap.m.Label({text: "Created On"}),
        new sap.ui.commons.TextField({value: "{createdOn}",
                            width:"200px",
                            editable: false,
                            }),

        new sap.m.Label({text: "Net Value"}),
        new sap.ui.commons.TextField({value: "{netValue}",
                            width:"200px",
                            }),

        new sap.m.Label({text: "Sales Organization"}),
        new sap.ui.commons.TextField({value: "{sOrg}",
                            width:"200px",
                            editable: false}),

        new sap.m.Label({text: "Sold-to-Party"}),
        new sap.ui.commons.TextField({value: "{customer}",
                            width:"200px"}),
    ]
});
```

Figure 7.3: SimpleForm to hold data

The title of the SimpleForm is defined and the content includes multiple Labels and TextFields to display information individually. Some Text-Fields have been made editable and some haven't. The editable ones allow you to edit the information.

Now that the SimpleForm has been created, let's add it to the page, as shown in Figure 7.4. The output is shown in Figure 7.5 and Figure 7.6. The property showNavButton is enabled and on clicking, it takes you back to the initial page.

```
var page2 = new sap.m.Page("page2", {
title: "Details of List Item",
showNavButton: true,
navButtonPress: function(){
    oApp.back();
},
content : simpleForm
});
```

Figure 7.4: Adding content to page 2

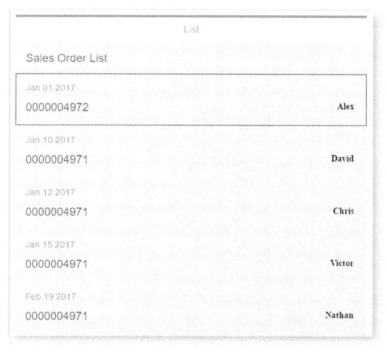

Figure 7.5: List Display

Figure 7.6: SimpleForm display

7.2 To search for items in a list

Create an App and add a page. Then, create a list and add it to the page. A new control called SearchField from sap.m library can be used which allows you to enter the data and provides results accordingly.

```
var order_list = new sap.m.List("purchaseOrder", {
});

var item1 = new sap.m.ObjectListItem({
intro: "{createdBy}",
title: "{PurchaseOrderNumber}",
number: "{companyCode}",
numberUnit: "Company Code",

});

order_list.bindItems({
    path: "/",
    template: item1,
});
```

Figure 7.7: Creating a list and adding items

Figure 7.7 shows the creation of a list with ObjectListItem and the binding of items to it.

SearchField has an event called "search" which enables you to enter data in order to search, as shown in Figure 7.8

```
var search = new sap.m.SearchField({
    placeholder: "Enter Order",
    showRefreshButton: true,
    liveChange: oController.order_search,
    search: oController.order_search,
});
```

Figure 7.8: Creating a search field

On a search event, the value entered is captured and stored in a variable. The filter control allows a filter for list binding. The FilterOperator filters depending on the operator, which is shown in Figure 7.9. The liveChange event triggers as soon as the data is entered in the Search-Field and displays the result instantly. The list display and liveChange for the output field can be seen in Figure 7.10 and Figure 7.11. Figure 7.12 shows the triggering of a search event.

```
order_search: function(oEvent) {
    var val = oEvent.getParameter("newValue");
    var filters = new Array();
    var oFilter = new sap.ui.model.Filter("PurchaseOrderNumber", sap.ui.model.FilterOperator.Contains, val);
    filters.push(oFilter);

    this.order_list = sap.ui.getCore().byId("purchaseOrder");
    this.order_list.getBinding("items").filter(filters);
    },
```

Figure 7.9: Filtering the list

Figure 7.10: List display with search field

Figure 7.11: LiveChange event

Figure 7.12: Search event

7.3   Sorting and grouping

The example in Figure 7.13 demonstrates sorting and grouping of items in a list.

Create a list and place it in a page. To sort a list, a control called Sorter from sap.ui.model library can be used. In this example, multiple items in an order are provided, that need to be sorted and grouped.

```
var oList= new sap.m.List({
    items: {
        path: "/",
        template: new sap.m.ObjectListItem("obj",{
            visible: true,
            title:"{item}",
            path: "item",
            }),

            sorter: new sap.ui.model.Sorter("order",false, function(oContext) {
            return { key: oContext.getProperty("order"),

            };
        })
    }
});
```

Figure 7.13: Sorting the list

127

Figure 7.13 shows the creation of a list and ObjectListItems along with binding, using a path. Sorter is defined, which allows grouping of items for every order and segregates the orders at the same time. The output can be seen in Figure 7.14.

Figure 7.14: Sorting and grouping

7.4 Application using a SplitApp

In this example, the master page is used to display a list of items and a detail page displays the details of items in the list.

Create a SplitApp and define a master page, and then add content to it.

```
var oSplitApp = new sap.m.SplitApp({});
    oSplitApp.placeAt("content");

var oMasterPage = new sap.m.Page("oMasterPage",{
    title:"Master Page",
    showFooter: true
    });

oSplitApp.addMasterPage(oMasterPage);

var oList = new sap.m.List("oList",{});

    oMasterPage.addContent(oList);
```

Figure 7.15: Adding a master page

The list type in the example in Figure 7.15 can be set to Navigation, which makes the list item clickable. On a click event, the details should appear on the detail page. Create a detail page with value holders to hold the details, as shown in Figure 7.16.

```
var oDetailPage = new sap.m.Page("oDetailPage",{
    title:"Detail Page",

        content: [ obj,
            new sap.m.Panel({
                content:[
                    new sap.ui.layout.form.SimpleForm({
                    editable:false,
                    content:[
                            new sap.m.Label("l1",{text:"Device"}),
                            new sap.ui.commons.TextField("i1",{value:"(name)",
                            editable: false}),
                            new sap.m.Label("l2",{text:"Manufacturer"}),
                            new sap.ui.commons.TextField("i2",{value:"(Manufacturer)",
                            editable: false}),
                            new sap.m.Label("l3",{text:"OS"}),
                            new sap.ui.commons.TextField("i3",{value:"(type)",
                            editable: false}),
                            new sap.m.Label("l5",{text:"Processor"}),
                            new sap.ui.commons.TextField("i5",{value:"(processor)",
                            editable: false}),
                            ]
                        })

                        ]

        })] });
    oSplitApp.addDetailPage(oDetailPage);
```

Figure 7.16: Creating a detail page

Figure 7.17 shows how to capture the data from the list and set it to SimpleForm on the detail page. Its output is shown in Figure 7.18.

```
var oList = new sap.m.List("oList",{});

    oMasterPage.addContent(oList);

oList.setModel(sap.ui.getCore().getModel("example"));
oList.bindItems("/", new sap.m.ObjectListItem({
        title:"{name}",
        intro:"{manufacturer}",
        number:"{windows}",
        numberUnit:"{processor}",
        type: sap.m.ListType.Navigation,
            press: function(event){

        var title = event.oSource.mProperties.title;
        sap.ui.getCore().byId("i1").setValue(title);

        var intro = event.oSource.mProperties.intro;
        sap.ui.getCore().byId("i5").setValue(intro);

        var number = event.oSource.mProperties.number;
        sap.ui.getCore().byId("i2").setValue(number);

        var numberUnit = event.oSource.mProperties.numberUnit;
        sap.ui.getCore().byId("i3").setValue(numberUnit);
        }
        }
        ));
```

Figure 7.17: List on a master page

Output

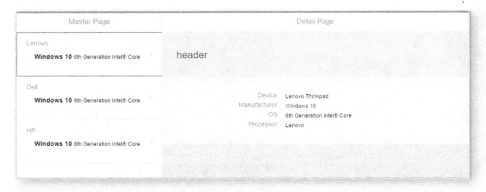

Figure 7.18: SplitApp

Split app creation

In this video, you will learn how to create a split app: *http://UI3.espresso-tutorials.com*

List on split app

In this video, you will learn how to create a list on split app: *http://UI4.espresso-tutorials.com*

7.5 To delete rows from a table

Create an App and add a page to it. Add a footer to the page and place a button in it which triggers the delete mode of the table rows, as shown in Figure 7.19.

```
var oApp= new sap.m.App({});
oApp.placeAt("content");

var page1 = new sap.m.Page({
    title:"Deleting a row from a Table",
    footer: new sap.m.Bar({

        contentRight: new sap.m.Button({
            text:"Delete",
            type:sap.m.ButtonType.Reject,
            press:function(event){
                oTable.setMode('Delete');
                }
            })
            })
        });
```

Figure 7.19: Adding a button to the bottom of a page

The button is placed in the footer by creating a bar control and determining its position. It can also be placed at the left or in the middle of the footer, and the button type is "reject".

To add a table to the page, Column and ColumnListItem can be used. On the click of a button, the delete mode is triggered and the delete event allows you to delete a row from the table.

The set mode defines the mode of control (SingleSelect, MultiSelect and Delete). Instead of Delete, SingleSelect or MultiSelect can be used. Figure 7.20 shows how the row is deleted from the table and its output is shown in Figure 7.21.

```
var oTable = new sap.m.Table({
    headerText:"Table Layout",
    delete: function(e){

        var content = e.getParameters().listItem.getBindingContext().sPath;
        content = content.slice(1);

                var d = oModel.getData();
                d.splice(content, 1);
                oModel.setData(d);


        }

    });

page1.addContent(oTable);
```

Figure 7.20: Creating a table and deleting rows

Output:

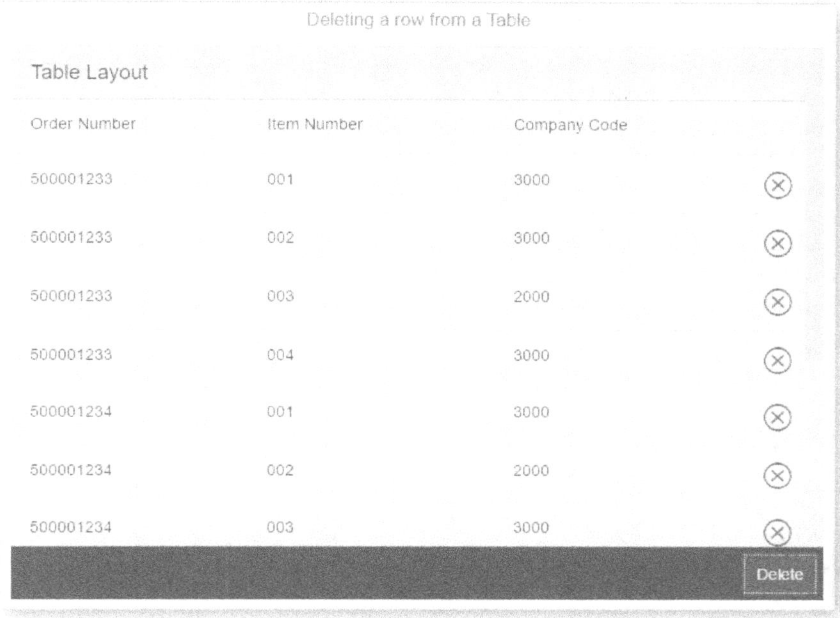

Figure 7.21: Deleting mode triggered on click of delete button

Clicking on the x symbol deletes the respective row from the table. Figure 7.22 shows the table from which item 001 and 002 of order 500001233 were deleted.

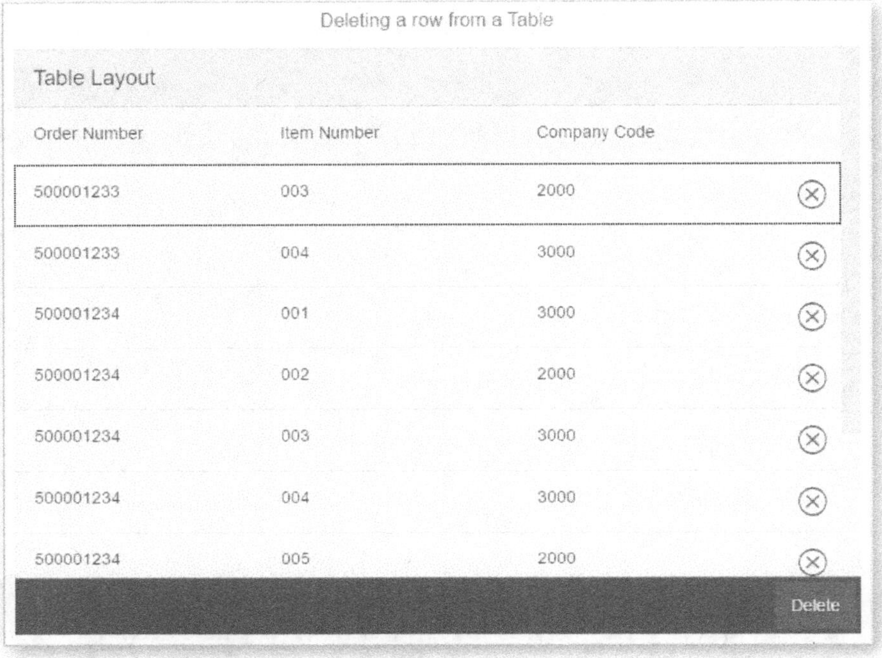

Figure 7.22: Table after deleting rows

8 Works Cited

STERN, J. (2013, May 29). *Cellphone Users Check Phones 150x/Day and Other Internet Fun Facts.* Retrieved from *http://abcnews.go.com: http://abcnews.go.com/blogs/technology/2013/05/cellphone-users-check-phones-150xday-and-other-internet-fun-facts/*

You have finished the book.

A   The Authors

Prem Manghnani is a very dynamic mobile application architect who has been working on mobile application technologies since their inception. With a great track record in the field of mobile applications, he has worked on multiple projects utilizing SAP Fiori and Neptune software application developments.

Seshu Reddy is a veteran in the field of SAP with over 20 years' experience. He has consulting experience in both technical and functional areas. Seshu has been working with a multitude of companies which offer a variety of SAP solutions such as functional and technical aspects, and UI5.

Sheshank Vyas has vast experience in the functional aspects of SAP and emerging mobility technologies. He has worked with multiple clients on various projects related to SAP implementation, support and mobility projects.

B Index

U

UI elements 24
UI inspector 23
UI inspector, UI elements 24

V

Views 31
    HTML views 33
    JSON views 32
    XML views 32

D Disclaimer

This publication contains references to the products of SAP SE.

SAP, R/3, SAP NetWeaver, Duet, PartnerEdge, ByDesign, SAP Busi-nessObjects Explorer, StreamWork, and other SAP products and ser-vices mentioned herein as well as their respective logos are trademarks or registered trademarks of SAP SE in Germany and other countries.

Business Objects and the Business Objects logo, BusinessObjects, Crystal Reports, Crystal Decisions, Web Intelligence, Xcelsius, and other Business Objects products and services mentioned herein as well as their respective logos are trademarks or registered trademarks of Busi-ness Objects Software Ltd. Business Objects is an SAP company.

Sybase and Adaptive Server, iAnywhere, Sybase 365, SQL Anywhere, and other Sybase products and services mentioned herein as well as their respective logos are trademarks or registered trademarks of Sybase, Inc. Sybase is an SAP company.

SAP SE is neither the author nor the publisher of this publication and is not responsible for its content. SAP Group shall not be liable for errors or omissions with respect to the materials. The only warranties for SAP Group products and services are those that are set forth in the express warranty statements accompanying such products and services, if any. Nothing herein should be construed as constituting an additional warr-anty.

More Espresso Tutorials Books

Michal Krawczyk:

SAP® SOA Integration – Enterprise Service Monitoring

▶ Tools for Monitoring SOA Scenarios

▶ Forward Error Handling (FEH) and Error Conflict Handler (ECH)

▶ Configuration Tips

▶ SAP Application Interface Framework (AIF) Customization Best Practices

▶ Detailed Message Monitoring and Reprocessing Examples

http://5077.espresso-tutorials.com

Kathi Kones:

SAP® List Viewer (ALV) – A Practical Guide for ABAP Developers

▶ Learn how to write a basic SAP ALV program

▶ Walk through the object-oriented control framework and function modules

▶ Get tips on adding sorting and grouping features

▶ Dive into how to add editable fields, events, and layout variants

http://5112.espresso-tutorials.com

Anurag Barua:

First Steps in SAP® Fiori

▶ SAP Fiori fundamentals and core components

▶ Instructions on how to create and enhance an SAP Fiori app

▶ Installation and configuration best practices

▶ Similarities and differences between SAP Fiori and Screen Personas

http://5126.espresso-tutorials.com

Jelena Perfiljeva:

What on Earth is an SAP® IDoc?

▶ Fundamentals of inbound and outbound IDoc interfaces and configuration

▶ Learn how to implement interfaces with ALE and EDI

▶ Troubleshoot common post-implementation challenges

▶ Quick reference guide to common IDoc transaction codes and reports

http://5130.espresso-tutorials.com

Paul Bakker & Rick Bakker:

How to Pass the SAP® ABAP Certification Exam

▶ Essential guide on how to pass the ABAP Associate Certification exam

▶ Expert ABAP certification tips

▶ Overview of certification exam topics

▶ Short and full-length practice exams with answer guides

http://5136.espresso-tutorials.com

Raquel Seville:

SAP® OpenUI5 for Mobile BI and Analytics

▶ Delve into the foundations of CSS, HTML5, and jQuery

▶ Learn how to build a seamless mobile BI app using SAP OpenUI5

▶ Use open source library d3.js to create custom data visualizations for bar, line, and pie charts

▶ Build web apps using real world scenarios and test layout options for different mobile devices

http://5173.espresso-tutorials.com

Robert Burdwell:

First Steps for Building SAP®UI5 Mobile Apps

▶ Introduction to mobile and SAP UI5 development

▶ Steps for building mobile apps in Eclipse, SAP Cloud Platform, and Microsoft Visual Studio

▶ How to deploy apps to multiple devices

▶ Advantages and disadvantages of using different environments

http://5176.espresso-tutorials.com